The Maximum Wage

**A Common-Sense Prescription for
Revitalizing America—by Taxing the Very Rich**

The Maximum Wage

A Common-Sense Prescription for Revitalizing America—by Taxing the Very Rich

By Sam Pizzigati

Illustrated by Howard Saunders

The Apex Press
New York

Copyright © 1992 by The Apex Press

The Apex Press (formerly New Horizons Press) is an imprint of the Council on International and Public Affairs, 777 United Nations Plaza, New York, New York 10017 (212/953-6920)

Library of Congress Cataloging-in-Publication Data:

Pizzigati, Sam.
      The maximum wage : a common-sense prescription for revitalizing America—
by taxing the very rich / by Sam Pizzigati : illustrated by Howard Saunders.
          p.   cm.
    ISBN 0-945257-45-7
    1. Income distribution—United States. 2. Wealth—United States.
I. Title.
HC110.I5P59 1992
339.2'2'0973—dc20   91-33410
                                                            CIP

Cover design by Howard Saunders
Typeset and printed in the United States of America

Table of Contents

An Introduction to
THE MAXIMUM WAGE

Poverty. We all know what to think about poverty. We're against it. Our nation, we all agree, would be a far better place to live if there were no poor people.

Wealth is a different story. Wealth—or, to be more specific, the uneven distribution of wealth—makes us uneasy. But who among us hasn't daydreamed about becoming wealthy? Who among us has never bought a lottery ticket?

Our chances of hitting a big lottery score are, of course, infinitessimal. Our chances of becoming rich—in any fashion—are equally remote. "The probability that anyone will rise from the lower 99 percent to the top 1 percent of the wealth distribution," says analyst Stanley Lebergott, "is less than 0.0002."[1] Yet we daydream on. We never dare imagine an alternative, never dare imagine what America might be like if there were no rich people.

Well, almost never. Down through the years, Americans have, at times, batted around the notion that this nation would be a better place to live if there were no very wealthy in our midst. In the nineteenth century, in fact, the biggest best-seller—after the *Bible* and *Ben-Hur*—was a novel that imagined an America without rich people. In the 1930s, what may well have been the biggest grassroots upsurge in United States history was inspired by a senator from Louisiana who wanted to "share the wealth."

How quaint these sentiments seem today. We don't talk about

sharing wealth any more. We don't generally see rich people as a problem. Maybe we should.

Rich people, the pages ahead will argue, are sapping the strength of America. Their continued presence is corrupting our democracy and strangling our economy. Their values are undermining our values. We would be better off, individually and as a nation, without them.

An America without rich people. An impossible dream? Maybe not. The pages ahead will both make the case for a rich people-free America—and offer a strategy to move us in that direction.

In Chapter One, we'll take a closer look at America's rich people problem and see just how high a price we pay for tolerating the presence of the very wealthy. In Chapter Two, we'll step back in time and trace the many struggles Americans have waged to cut the rich down to democratic size.

These struggles against great disparities in wealth, in the end, all failed. Chapter Three explores that failure and offers a proposal that just might bring future success. This proposal, what we have dubbed the "Ten Times Rule," would, if enacted, cut taxes significantly for all Americans—except the very richest—and start a social chain reaction that would enhance nearly every aspect of contemporary American life. Chapter Four describes how this social chain reaction would likely unfold.

Finally, in Chapter Five, we examine what it would take, politically, to enact the Ten Times Rule and downsize America's great fortunes.

How great are these fortunes? On this question, we begin.

---

1. Quoted in Jennifer L. Hochschild, *What's Fair?: American Beliefs about Distributive Justice* (Cambridge: Harvard University Press, 1981), p. 13.

1. The Rich People Problem

Over a generation ago, in the 1950s, economists didn't waste much sleep contemplating the rich people problem. Inequities of income and wealth just didn't seem very important. Working people appeared to be more economically comfortable than ever before, and the days of wealthy robber barons seemed misty memories from a distant past. Some economists even argued that wide disparities in wealth were actually disappearing from the American scene. Industrial economies, maintained the eminent Simon Kuznets in a landmark 1955 address, generate considerable inequality in their early days, significantly less as they mature.[1]

These days, no one argues that great fortunes are disappearing. In today's "mature" American economy, wealth remains as unevenly divided as ever.

How unevenly divided? That isn't easy to say. We just don't know for sure how wealthy the wealthy are. Federal law does require the Internal Revenue Service to report tax collection results, and these reports do produce some useful data. The federal Securities and Exchange Commission reports the executive salaries of companies that trade on stock exchanges, and this information is helpful, too. But no government agency is legally mandated to track wealth pure and simple.[2] Unlike poor people, rich people aren't required to report to public agencies where statistics can be gathered about their holdings.

"The rich," notes one of their critics, "are probably the most inaccessible people in the country to researchers."[3]

Scholars never cease to be amazed, as Henry Phelps Brown of the London School of Economics has put it, that "so few facts have been gathered about so prominent and contentious a subject as wealth."[4]

The few facts we do have are dramatic enough. According to 1983 figures from the Joint Economic Committee of Congress, the richest one half of 1 percent of America's households own 28 percent of the nation's wealth. These well-endowed households average $10 million per family.

More recently, IRS researchers, working from estate tax return data, have concluded that 941,000 American families had a "net worth"—the total of assets less debts—of $1 million or more in 1986.[5] The $4.3 trillion in personal wealth held by the richest 3.3 million Americans in 1986 actually exceeded America's $4.1 trillion Gross National Product.[6]

In 1988, the U.S. Census Bureau surveyed a cross-section of American households and tried to calculate wealth by first totalling the value of bank accounts, stocks, bonds, motor vehicles, homes, and assorted other real estate, then subtracting mortgages, debts, and outstanding bills.[7] This Census Bureau study concluded that the wealthiest 3 percent of all households hold 27 percent of the $8.4 trillion in net worth of American households. But the author of the study noted that the Census Bureau figures understate the wealth of the wealthiest Americans, mainly because the Census Bureau's net worth figures didn't tally the value of art, antiques, and other forms of wealth that rich people have far more of than anyone else.[8]

Over the years, other analysts have made similar points. "Much of the net worth of the wealthy reflects marketable assets, such as securities and real estate, which are passsed on by inheritance from one generation to the next," economist Arthur Okun once noted. "In contrast, middle-class wealth typically takes the form of furniture, household equipment, and automobiles, which are worn out over the years rather than bequeathed to heirs."[9]

Control over America's "marketable assets" belongs overwhelmingly to a very small group of Americans at the lofty peak of the nation's economic pyramid. The richest 1 percent of Americans own, for instance, 60 percent of the nation's corporate stock.

The numbers become even more striking when you consider the holdings of those few Americans at the very tip of the nation's economic pyramid. In 1986, after *Forbes* magazine profiled America's 482 richest individuals and families, economist Lester Thurow calculated that their $166 billion in business net worth gives these very rich Americans effective control over "40 percent of all fixed, nonresidential private capital in the United States."[10]

In all, says *Fortune* magazine, America currently sports 58 billionaires, another thousand fortunate souls in the $100 million league, and several tens of thousands others with at least $10 million.[11] The average American family, meanwhile, has a net worth of $35,752, and three-quarters of that total reflects home value.[12]

Income—the annual receipts from wages, salary, dividends, rent, interest, and profits—is easier to measure than wealth, thanks largely to the IRS. Not surprisingly, the vast disparities

> *America sports over 1,000 fortunate souls worth over $100 million. The average American family, meanwhile, has a net worth of $35,752.*

in income the IRS reports reflect America's vast disparities in wealth. In 1990, notes economist Robert Reich, "the top fifth of working Americans took home more money than the other four-fifths put together—the highest portion in postwar history."[13] All quite true, but the real income chasm isn't between the top fifth of Americans and everybody else. The largest income chasm lies between the rich and the non-rich.

Who are the rich? *Money* magazine put that question to its upscale readership (average family income: $66,000) in 1990. About nine in 10 *Money* readers said an American would have to

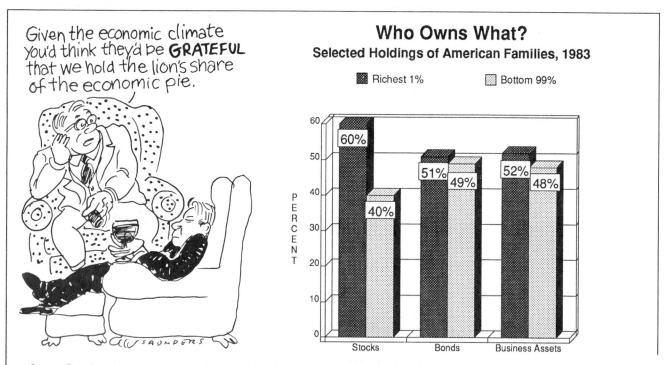

Given the economic climate you'd think they'd be **GRATEFUL** that we hold the lion's share of the economic pie.

Who Owns What?
Selected Holdings of American Families, 1983

■ Richest 1%   ▨ Bottom 99%

Stocks: 60% / 40%
Bonds: 51% / 49%
Business Assets: 52% / 48%

PERCENT

Source: Data from Lawrence Mishel and David M. Frankel, *The State of Working America, 1990-91 Edition*, p. 154.

"be among the top 1% of wage earners—those earning $100,000 or more—to be considered rich."[14]

Actually, according to the statistics, a family had to have an income of at least $208,000 to make it into America's richest 1 percent in 1990. The "average" rich person in 1990's top 1 percent pulled in, before taxes, $549,000.[15]

In the 1980s, the gap between the top 1 percent and everybody else widened considerably. Over the course of the decade, the incomes of the upper 1 percent grew by 74 percent. The $233,322 average income *increase* registered by America's richest 1 percent

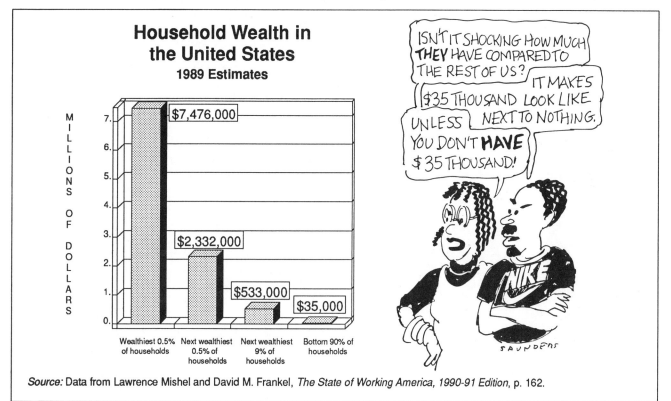

Household Wealth in the United States
1989 Estimates

MILLIONS OF DOLLARS

- Wealthiest 0.5% of households: $7,476,000
- Next wealthiest 0.5% of households: $2,332,000
- Next wealthiest 9% of households: $533,000
- Bottom 90% of households: $35,000

Source: Data from Lawrence Mishel and David M. Frankel, *The State of Working America, 1990-91 Edition*, p. 162.

in the 1980s, in fact, nearly doubled the average *income* of the next best-off 4 percent. To put the matter even more starkly, the typical income gain of America's wealthiest 1 percent in the 1980s was "more than 5 times the average family income in 1990."[16]

By 1990, adds the Center on Budget and Policy Priorities, the top 1 percent of the population could claim "as much after-tax income as the bottom 40 percent."[17]

Statistics actually understate the income disparities between ordinary Americans and America's wealthiest 1 percent. Those working American families whose incomes did rise in the 1980s

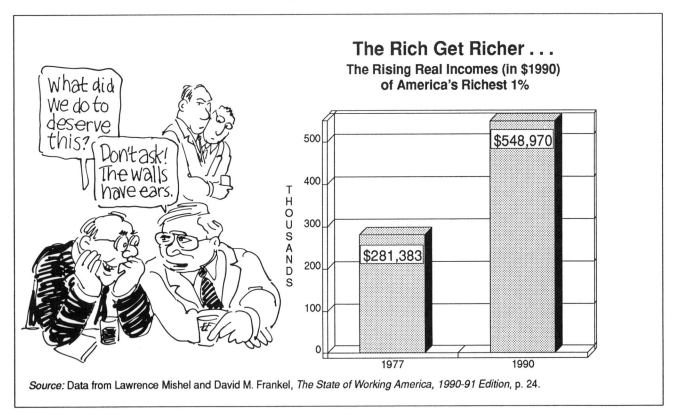

The Rich Get Richer . . .
The Rising Real Incomes (in $1990) of America's Richest 1%

Source: Data from Lawrence Mishel and David M. Frankel, *The State of Working America, 1990-91 Edition*, p. 24.

owed their higher earnings almost entirely to wives who worked more and more hours outside the home. But as the hours wives worked outside the home rose, so did family expenses for transportation, clothes, and child care.[18]

The wealthy face no such expense squeeze on their income. The richest 1 percent of Americans rake in nearly half their income from financial assets—rent, dividends, interest—and this income, unlike the income non-rich Americans earn by working harder and longer, doesn't come with any strings.

All these income statistics can become numbing. The dis-

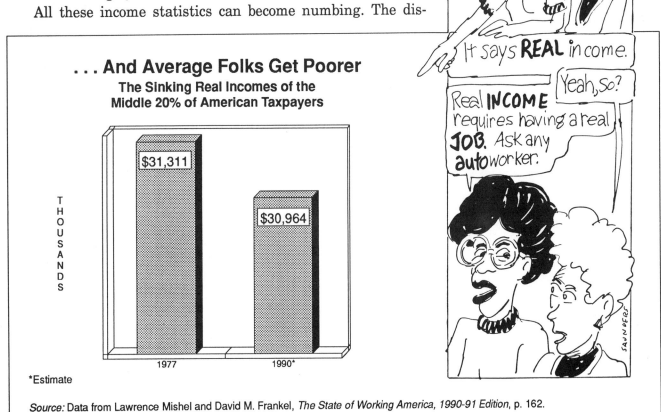

. . . And Average Folks Get Poorer
The Sinking Real Incomes of the Middle 20% of American Taxpayers

$31,311 (1977) $30,964 (1990*)

T H O U S A N D S

*Estimate

Source: Data from Lawrence Mishel and David M. Frankel, *The State of Working America, 1990-91 Edition*, p. 162.

parities are so wide, the numbers so high, that it often becomes difficult to visualize the human reality the statistics are actually describing. Over the years, several economists have taken stabs at explaining, in easy-to-understand terms, just how vast America's income differences have become. Economist Paul Samuelson's description, now 30 years old, remains perhaps the most vivid:

> If we made an income pyramid out of a child's blocks, with each layer portraying $1,000 of income, the peak would be far higher than the Eiffel Tower, but almost all of us would be within a yard of the ground.[19]

There are those who aren't bothered by this gaping difference. Indeed, some people nearly exult in it. Great wealth, these commentators maintain, is the fountainhead of civilization, a buffer against cultural uniformity and monotony.[20] Civilization, the argument continues, requires a leisure class because "work tires the body and blunts the intellect."[21]

"The rich make life more interesting: they are a luxury a civilized society should be able to afford," writes William Davis, a chronicler of the rich and famous.[22] "Walk around any museum and look at the treasures they have left us, and ask yourself what there would be to see if Communism had arrived four centuries earlier."[23]

"The world," concludes Davis, "would be a poorer place if the rich ceased to exist."[24]

These gushy justifications for wealth have never resonated too well in American ears. Most Americans, even rich Americans, are somewhat embarrassed by great fortunes. Indeed, the rich people Americans most respect are those who downplay the cosmic significance of their riches.

"The money doesn't matter—not after the first million," philanthropist Joseph Hirshhorn once said. "How could it? You can't wear more than two shirts in a day, or eat more than three meals."[25]

To rich people like Hirshhorn, and their admirers, great disparities in wealth are simply the price we must pay, the burden we must bear, for a free and productive society. "That some should be rich," as Abraham Lincoln once noted, "shows that others may become rich and hence is encouragement to industry and enterprise."[26] Eliminate the ability to amass wealth and you eliminate the incentive to achieve. Warned Andrew Mellon, the U.S. Secretary of the Treasury for a dozen years after World War I: "when initiative is crippled by legislation or by a tax system which denies the taxpayer to receive a reasonable share of his earnings, then he will no longer exert himself and the country will be deprived of the energy on which its continued greatness depends."[27]

The great British economist John Maynard Keynes was no great fan of great fortunes. But even Keynes considered the chase after wealth a very necessary evil. The capacity to make money, Keynes felt, shuttles "some dangerous human proclivities into comparatively safe channels." Absent the opportunity to make money, "these proclivities might find their outlets in cruelty, the reckless pursuit of personal power, and other forms of aggrandizement."[28]

In short, for a variety of reasons, we need rich people.

But do we? Is the presence of rich people truly essential to our well-being?

Our society seldom makes this reckoning. Perhaps it's time

Eliminate the ability to amass great wealth, rich people have argued down through the years, and you eliminate the incentive to achieve.

we did. What exactly is the price we pay for the privilege of having rich people among us? What impact do rich people actually have on our lives and our nation?

Let's try to answer these questions. Let's examine the impact of the wealthy on three distinctly important aspects of American life: our democracy, our economy, and our character.

Wealth and Democracy

In 1757, one of early America's wealthiest men sought a seat in Virginia's colonial legislature, the House of Burgesses. The gentleman left nothing to chance. To guarantee his election, this aspiring politician bought 28 gallons of rum, 50 gallons of rum punch, 34 gallons of wine, 46 gallons of beer, and two gallons of cider. Contemporary observers were impressed. There were, after all, only 391 voters in young George Washington's district.[29]

In 1884, one of the wealthiest men of his time, Henry B. Payne, wanted to become the next United States senator from Ohio. Payne's son Oliver, the treasurer of Standard Oil, did his best to help. Just before the election for Ohio's seat, son Oliver "sat at a desk in a Columbus hotel with a stack of bills in front of him, paying for the votes of the state legislators," who then elected U.S. senators.[30]

In 1980, the Republican National Committee, the National Republican Senatorial Committee, and the National Republican Congressional Committee spent about six times more on electioneering than did their Democratic Party counterparts.[31] The spending paid off. The 1980 elections swept into power the first Republican Senate majority in a generation and gave newly elected President Ronald Reagan enough congressional support to enact unprecedented tax cuts for the wealthy and budget cuts for the programs serving everybody else. Democrats in Congress offered amazingly tepid resistance to the Reagan Revolution's giveaway to the wealthy, at least partly because, some charged, the Democrats were chasing after the same deep-pockets contributors who had handed the GOP its whopping 1980 fundraising edge.

Pick an era, any era. Wealth always makes its presence felt. Democracy is supposed to be a free-flowing clash of ideas. The best ideas—the ideas that benefit the most people—are supposed to emerge triumphant. But wealth tilts the scales. Wealth makes some ideas—and the candidates who espouse them—more likely to succeed than other ideas, even if the ideas backed by that wealth are not in society's best interests.

Right from our republic's earliest days, Americans have worried constantly about the dangerous impact of great wealth on democracy.

Down through the years, Americans have worried constantly about the dangerous impact of great wealth on democracy. In 1776, artisans from Philadelphia tried unsuccessfully to have Pennsylvania's new state constitution declare that "an enormous Proportion of Property vested in a few Individuals is dangerous to the Rights, and destructive of the Common Happiness of Mankind; and therefore any free State hath a Right by its Laws to discourage the Possession of such Property."[32] Benjamin Franklin, another Philadelphian, "argued that no man ought to own more property than needed for his livelihood; the rest, by right, belonged to the state."[33]

A few years later, in the debates over the adoption of the Constitution, James Madison called "the unequal and various distribution of property" the "most common and durable source" of factions.[34] In 1792, Madison argued that the young nation needed laws to "reduce extreme wealth toward a state of mediocrity, and raise indigence towards a state of comfort."[35] The nation, of course, never enacted those laws. "Immoderate" accumulations of wealth did appear and did, as Madison feared, distort the democratic process.

"We can either have democracy in this country," future Supreme Court Justice Louis Brandeis concluded six generations after Madison, "or we can have great wealth concentrated in the hands of a few, but we can't have both."[36]

The handwringing over wealth in politics continues unabated today. Despite decades of reforms meant to prevent wealthy special interests from buying elections, the weight of the wealthy has never seemed heavier. Members of Congress now routinely retire in disgust, complaining bitterly about the inordinate amounts of time they have to spend soliciting contributions from wealthy constituents. To finance the cost of a typical campaign, an average senator must now "raise $15,000 each and every week of a full six-year term."[37] Those financially well-endowed individuals who make that fundraising easier always find a welcome on Capitol Hill. Savings and Loan kingpin Charles Keating, who contributed hundreds of thousands of dollars to political candidates in the 1980s, separated thousands of middle-class people from their life savings—and then collected a small herd of U.S. senators to run interference for him when regulators came snooping.

Many angry Americans believe we need stronger campaign finance reforms. Laws have been introduced that would outlaw political action committees or make congressional campaigns publicly financed or force TV networks to offer candidates free air-time. Ironically, some of these proposals seek to undo earlier reforms. Political action committees, for instance, emerged as a reform alternative in the Watergate era. Americans in the 1970s were outraged by the sight of wealthy individuals contributing unholy sums to candidate campaign coffers. Reformers successfully limited the amounts individuals could contribute to campaigns and boosted the political action committee as a much healthier alternative. PACs, reformers argued, would pool contributions from many different individuals. With PACs in place and large individual contributions to candidates banned, reformers believed, campaigns would be far less dependent on the largess of big-time special interest wealth and power.

It didn't work out that way. Rich people simply changed the way they did politics. A wealthy individual interested in subsidizing a candidacy first wrote out the personal contribution allowed by law, then called up a dozen wealthy friends and asked them to follow suit. PACs, meanwhile, emerged in industry after industry and funneled candidates huge amounts in contributions. So why not simply abolish PACs and further limit individual contributions? That could be done—but wealth would simply seek other political outlets. If giving generously to individual candidates became impossible, rich people would instead give more to the candidates' political parties. If that avenue were closed, rich people might start bankrolling political training institutes that would outfit their favorite candidates with the high-tech skills and research they need to smother their opposition.

And if reformers were to ban these training centers, rich people might perhaps buy the local area's daily newspaper and editorialize on behalf of their favorite candidate. And what then would be the appropriate campaign finance reform? Repeal the First Amendment?

In hydraulic systems, water seeks its own level, no matter what you do. In political systems, wealth will have an impact, no

> *Despite decades of reforms meant to prevent wealthy special interests from buying elections, the political weight of the wealthy has never seemed heavier.*

matter what you do. We can, as a nation, continue to dabble in election reform after reform. But the reforms that seem most effective will only maintain their effectiveness until wealth figures out an alternate route to influence. The heart of democracy's rich people problem isn't inadequate regulation. It's the presence of rich people themselves. As long as a society is "free," then rich people will be free to influence political decisions disproportionately—and politics will reflect the agendas of rich people.

Society's choice is stark. Either we limit political freedom of expression—which no good American wants—or we try to limit wealth.

And if we continue on our current course? Let's be candid. If we continue to practice politics as usual, the prospects for our democracy are not good. We are caught in a depoliticizing cycle. Average Americans face real economic problems, but politicians seldom challenge the economic status quo at the root of those problems—because that would place them outside the bounds of conventional politics, as defined by the agendas of rich people. Outside these bounds, there are no financial support systems that allow a candidate to compete effectively. Candidates who want to win must, by necessity, narrow their vision.

The more politics narrows, the less politics interest average Americans. They vote, but nothing ever seems to change. So why bother?

The percentage of Americans who vote has been declining for decades now, as analysts have noted repeatedly. But that decline doesn't run evenly across the income spectrum. Wealthier people have not lost the voting habit. Low- and middle-income people have. In 1990, those voters in households making under $30,000 made up just 32 percent of the voting electorate. These same households make up over 60 percent of the total population.[38]

Nations can survive if citizens choose not to participate in the political process. But they cease to be democracies. We as a nation are headed in a nondemocratic direction. The presence and power of rich people are pushing us that way. The crisis of our democracy is, at root, a rich people problem. We can take rich people on—and start a new politics—or we can risk our democracy. There simply is no other option.

As Alexis de Tocqueville put it a century and a half ago: "Those who believe that complete equality can be established in a permanent way in the political world without introducing at the same time a certain equality in civil society, seem to me to commit a great error."[39]

> *The heart of democracy's rich people problem isn't inadequate regulation of the electoral process. It's the very presence of rich people.*

Wealth and the Economy

Do rich people strengthen our economy—or weaken it?

Over the course of the twentieth century, two opposing answers have vied for the allegiance of average Americans.

The wealthy and their friends have argued that the richer some people get, the better off the rest of us will be. The more money rich people accumulate, the more money will be available for investments and innovations that create jobs and economic security. When the rich prosper, everybody benefits.

This "cow-dung" approach to economics—you feed the cow so the flies can eat—has never quite won over the American people. Most Americans just aren't comfortable with the notion that their economic lot in life depends on what "trickles down" from above.

The alternate view of what works best for market economies starts from a totally different set of assumptions. In this alternate view, the key to prosperity isn't the wealth of the rich. It's the purchasing power of working people.

Want to keep the economy humming? Put dollars in the pockets of average citizens, not rich people. Regular working people will take those dollars and spend them on honey hams, lawn chairs, and washers and dryers. Their demand for products and services will keep businesses neck-deep in orders. Jobs will be plentiful. Everyone will benefit.

Put those same dollars in the pockets of rich people, on the other hand, and jobs will be less plentiful. Rich people, to be sure, do spend prodigiously on products and services, and this spending does create jobs. But not all the dollars in the deep pockets of the very wealthy go for products and services. Their pockets are simply too deep. America's multi-millionaires could shop 'til they drop every day of their lives and still boast quite tidy fortunes. You can, after all, only spend so much on sushi, tummy tucks, and yachts.

And after the tummy tucks, what happens to all those dollars left over in the tidy fortunes of the very wealthy? These idle dollars invariably flow into speculative investments that add no real value—or jobs—to the economy. Rich people simply don't see money in the same terms as the rest of us. We can't afford to risk any significant chunk of our savings. They can. We depend on every dollar we earn. They don't. Rich people can afford to chase speculative investments that offer big returns—and so they do.

"Whenever wealth disparity rises," economist Ravi Batra writes, "speculation rises with it."[40]

Batra is only the latest in a long line of economists to emphasize the link between great disparities in wealth, speculation, and subsequent economic collapse. His 1980s best-seller, *The*

Great Depression of 1990, argues that "recessions are caused by unequal distribution of income."[41] All great depressions, notes Batra, "have been preceded by great speculative manias triggered by high wealth disparity."[42]

Nearly 60 years ago, Franklin D. Roosevelt sounded a similar theme in his 1932 campaign for the Presidency. America's top economic problem, Roosevelt told a depression-wracked nation, wasn't "an insufficiency of capital." America's problem was "an insufficient distribution of buying power coupled with an oversufficient speculation in production."[43] In other words, the problem wasn't that rich people didn't have enough money to invest. The problem was that everyone else didn't have enough to buy.

Contemporary economists like Ravi Batra define depressions as recessions coupled with a financial collapse. In their analysis, as the rich become richer and wealth concentrates in fewer hands, more people are left with few or no assets. That reality increases the demand for loans, but the borrowers who get those loans are less credit-worthy. The number of banks with questionable loans rises. The stage is set for collapse.[44]

"In short," sums up Batra, "the concentration of wealth has two pernicious effects on the economy: it increases the number of banks with shaky loans, and fuels the speculative fever in which eventually even the banking industry is caught."[45]

Economist Jeff Faux sees the speculative fever of the 1980s in far less apocalyptic terms. What speculation generates, Faux argues, are missed opportunities for meaningful economic growth. The 1980s, says Faux, saw "a shift of capital from productive investment to financial speculation."[46] Over the course of the decade, Faux notes, "resources were squandered that should have been used to initiate and support an economic revival in the

A long line of economists has emphasized the link between great disparities in wealth, speculation, and eventual economic collapse.

1990s."[47]

If the rationale for great fortunes reflected reality—if the rich could be counted on to invest their fortunes in initiatives that would leave the rest of us better off—then the squandering Faux describes should never have taken place. But rich people did squander away the opportunities of the 1980s. The nation's infrastructure did waste away while rich people bid mega-millions for Rembrandts.

We shouldn't be surprised. It's not that rich people are inherently evil—or even short-sighted. We would behave the same way rich people do if we had their riches. Think about the $2 bettor who stumbles into a totally unexpected $100 daily double. How many times does the lucky winner turn around and bet that $100 foolishly away on the next few races? Our bettor didn't really earn that $100. It's less than "real." Lucky bettors routinely risk their winnings in ways they would never risk a paycheck.

For rich people, life is one longshot winner after another. Rich people "have money to burn." So they burn it. They risk it. Wouldn't you? What would give you more pleasure, speculating on an investment that might double your money in a year or putting your money into a predictable and eminently lifeless CD? If you could afford the risk, wouldn't you take it? If it didn't really matter if the money you risked were lost, wouldn't you take the risk? You wouldn't have anything to lose.

That's the position rich people are in. They have, economically speaking, nothing to lose but money—and they already have far more of that than they know what to do with. The rest of us, on the other hand, have plenty to lose when rich people play games with money. When their speculative houses crash, we're the ones left in the rubble. We as a society don't let our children play with matches. Why do we let rich people play with fortunes?

We are speaking here in broad economic terms. Speculation. Purchasing power. Recession. Depression. These are all phenomena that work at a grand, societal level. But, over recent years, more and more economists have begun looking at the impact rich people have on the smaller picture, on the building blocks of the modern economy, individual business enterprises. And what these economists have found is deeply troubling. Vast disparities of wealth within a business enterprise, these economists are concluding, undermine our nation's very economic foundation.

The typical American corporation is and always has been a colossal hierarchical bureaucracy. At the top of the corporate economic pyramid sits a tiny group of well-paid executives who call the corporate shots, at the bottom a vast army of production-line workers who are monitored but never consulted. These immense corporate bureaucracies move slowly. Marching orders are generated at the top and relayed to the troops through level upon level of middle management.

Today, almost all economic analysts believe, America can no longer afford such bureaucratic inertia. To compete successfully in the modern, wildly competitive international economic environment, a corporation must be flexible enough to turn on a dime. The modern corporation must have its ear to the ground, must be ever on the watch for new market trends or new, more productive ways to do business.

All this places a premium on information. In the modern business enterprise, information needs to flow freely. Top executives need to know—quickly—whatever changing market trends the company's salespeople are picking up. Ideas for streamlining

We non-rich have plenty to lose when rich people play games with money. When speculative houses crash, we're the ones left in the rubble.

production need to move speedily from workers to managers. The modern corporation, analysts believe, must welcome and encourage employee ideas and move these ideas rapidly into the decision-making loop.

The standard hierarchical corporate pyramid, of course, frustrates this ideal information flow. In the standard top-down hierarchy, any idea from below must run an obstacle course of bureaucracy before receiving any serious consideration by top-echelon corporate decision-makers. And that same bureaucracy tends to isolate the top echelons from real-world trends and changes.

The solution? Management theorists agree, almost to an MBA, that corporations must flatten their pyramidal structures, narrow the distance between on-line workers and corporate decision-makers, and create new corporate cultures where employees are encouraged to think and information is shared.

These words of wisdom have become staples on the business lecture circuit. No serious business leader in America today openly challenges this new management paradigm. Corporate leaders themselves, notes Harvard analyst Charles Heckscher, are even leading the rhetorical charge against hierarchy. The new language of management, he adds, "increasingly celebrates involvement, creativity, individual autonomy, participation, even 'empowering' employees to use their own initiative."[48]

The consensus for change in corporate America runs deep. Every day, every week, corporate workshops and training seminars are working overtime to inculcate new generations of corporate suits in more open, less hierarchical behaviors. And yet, in actual corporate workplaces, precious little has actually changed. Hierarchical pyramids still reign supreme.

"Only a tiny fraction [of corporations] have instituted widespread autonomous team structures," says Harvard's Heckscher, "and even these have not fundamentally challenged the overall hierarchy."[49]

Why can't corporations restructure? Corporations can't restructure because steep hierarchical pyramids aren't just anachronistic hangovers from a bygone age. In contemporary American economic life, corporate hierarchies serve a real purpose. Hierarchies are income-maintenance programs for rich people.

In hierarchies, after all, each level of bureaucracy must be compensated at a higher rate than the level below. The more levels, the higher the compensation at the summit. Any serious attempt to flatten the corporate pyramid would immediately jeopardize the lush compensation at the top.

Business leaders, naturally, seldom acknowledge this inconvenient reality. Corporations only offer top executives lush salary and benefit packages, business leaders argue, because the "market" values executive expertise. If you want top corporate talent, you have to pay the going rate.

This argument strikes Peter Drucker, America's most prominent management theorist, as "nonsense" pure and simple. The market, notes Drucker, does not justify immense corporate salaries. "Every executive knows perfectly well," says Drucker, "that it is the internal logic of a hierarchical structure that explains them."[50]

Executive compensation, adds economist John Kenneth Galbraith, is "a function not of market valuation but of tradition, hierarchical position and bureaucratic power."[51]

"The foreman has to get $15,000 after fringes or $20,000 in-

> *In contemporary American economic life, corporate hierarchies serve a real purpose. Hierarchies are income-maintenance programs for rich people.*

cluding fringes," Peter Drucker explained some years ago. "And each level above the foreman has to get at least 40 percent more it is believed. If there are 30 levels, then the top man has to get $500,000 plus, not because this is his 'market value,' but because otherwise the foreman could not be paid his $15,000."[52]

By the same token, of course, if those 30 levels were narrowed down, the top executive would not get his $500,000. Is it just coincidence that campaigns against corporate hierarchy have made so little headway?

Meanwhile, the overseas rivals of American corporations are making plenty of headway—in international economic competition. These rivals, interestingly enough, do not tolerate the huge income differentials so typical in the American corporate world.

The figures are stunning. The average CEO of a large U.S. corporation makes 35 times the wage of the average manufacturing employee in the United States. In Japan, the ratio is 15-1, in Europe 20-1.[53] In the fiercely competitive world auto industry, the comparisons are more vivid still. "In the early 1980s," write Mark Green and John Berry, "the chairman of Nissan Motors made $140,000 annually, the top ten officers at Renault, the French auto firm, earned $100,000 a year on average, yet the chairmen of GM and Ford at the same time earned about a million dollars annually. American auto executives receive 36 times the pay of their blue-collar workers, while the equivalent Japanese executive pulls down only seven times as much as his blue-collar workers."[54]

Since the early 1980s, the compensation margin between American executives and their counterparts abroad has actually widened. Over the last decade, U.S. corporate compensation has jumped almost three times faster than Japanese compensation and over four times faster than West German corporate compensation.

In 1989, top Japanese CEOs averaged $352,000 in pay, benefits, and perks. In the United States, the comparable top execs averaged $3.3 million[55]—at a time when Japanese corporations were running rings around their American competitors at every turn.

Any wonder that in 1986 Richard Darman, then deputy Secretary of the Treasury, called the conventional American business establishment "bloated, risk-averse, inefficient and

CEOs and Workers
An International Compensation Comparison

Source: Data from Joani Nelson-Horchler, "What's Your Boss Worth?" *The Washington Post*, August 6, 1990, p. D3.

unimaginative." Executives paid $1 million a year devote less time to research and development, said Darman, than "they spend reviewing their golf scores."[56]

One scholar, Warner Woodworth, has compiled an all-star list of horror stories that demonstrate just how bloated and inefficient the modern corporation has become:

- In 1986, John Nevin of Firestone took home $6,355,000, a 71 percent increase over the previous year, despite a 7.6 percent drop in Firestone sales, layoffs that had dropped the Firestone workforce from 107,000 to 55,000, and union wage concessions that had dropped the hourly rate as low as $3.65 an hour.[57]

- ITT Chairman Rand Araskog pulled in $4,255,000 in 1986, 66 percent more than his previous year's take-home, despite a 14.2 percent corporate sales slump.[58]

- Robert Formon of E. F. Hutton saw his cash compensation jump 23 percent in 1986, to $1.2 million. In the same year, Formon pled guilty to 2,000 counts of federal mail and wire fraud and watched company earnings drop 17.1 percent.[59]

Outrages like these leave the corporate rank and file something less than eager to devote much psychic energy to cooperative efforts to improve "efficiency" or "productivity." The bloated salaries at the top of the corporate pyramid, salaries that bear no relationship whatsoever to contribution, make a mockery of the rhetoric of collaboration and teamwork. Indeed, the inherent "team" nature of corporate enterprise makes mammoth executive salaries totally illegitimate as meaningful awards for performance. In a modern economy, analysts point out, "all results are the product of team labor," and, in this context, "there is no satis-factory way of isolating any one person's contribution"[60]—even a top executive's.

If corporations truly want to expand their "team," if corpora-tions want to tap the ideas and insights of rank-and-file employees, then their compensation systems must begin to en-courage a teamwork sensibility, and that means smaller income differentials within the corporation. That means corporations must stop manufacturing rich people.

Wealth and Character

Inequality, an Oxford philosopher once noted, "has a tenden-cy to produce envy, which is a disagreeable state of mind and leads people to do disagreeable things."[61]

The great moral prophets have always understood the power of wealth to make life disagreeable. Back in biblical times, this instinctive distaste for inequality engendered the jubilee, an am-bitious attempt to erase, every 50 years, the accumulated economic power that one person may gain over another. Com-mands *Leviticus:*

> And ye shall hallow the fiftieth year, and proclaim liberty throughout all the land unto all the inhabitants thereof; it shall be a jubilee unto you; and ye shall return every man unto his possession, and ye shall return every man unto his family.[62]

"The profit of the earth is for all," added another ancient com-mentator in *Ecclesiastes,*[63] but all never seemed to share in the profit. Rich people trod mightily the ancient world, lusting after wealth, monopolizing the resources of their day, inviting the cen-

The bloated salaries at the top of the corporate pyramid, salaries that bear no relationship to contribution, make a mockery of the rhetoric of collaboration.

sure of contemporary preachers.

"It is easier for a camel to pass through the eye of a needle," taught one, "than for a rich man to enter the Kingdom of God."[64]

Similar sentiments abound throughout the New Testament. Notes one biblical scholar: "Every time Jesus offers an opinion about riches, it is negative. Every time he teaches about the use of wealth, he counsels disciples to give it away."[65]

Over time, these ancient teachings began to lose something in the translation. By the 18th century, the individual who lusted after riches was no longer automatically suspect, as long as those riches went for noble causes. Advised the point man for Methodism, John Wesley: "Make all you can, save all you can, give all you can."

Wesley's three-sided formula hasn't quite survived the centuries. In modern America, notes scholar Thomas Schmidt, too many Americans "appear to have concluded that two out of three is not bad."[66] Americans today rush to make and save—and keep. We chase after wealth with a single-mindedness that frightens our most thoughtful observers.

"No matter what their income," writes *Harpers* editor Lewis Lapham, "a depressing number of Americans believe that if only they had twice as much, they would inherit the estate of happiness promised them by the Declaration of Independence."[67]

This isn't to say that Americans are oblivious to the corrupting influences of wealth. Far from it. Every Sunday, millions of Americans nod in approval when ministers thunder from a thousand pulpits that what counts in life are the values that money can't buy. A 1990 *Fortune* magazine poll found that few Americans consider money the best yardstick for evaluating what their lives are truly worth. Only 20 percent of Americans say money adequately measures the success of their lives. Far higher numbers of Americans place a premium on having enjoyable work (86 percent), happy children (84 percent), or a good marriage (69 percent).[68]

Americans, by and large, would also probably agree with F. Scott Fitzgerald's contention that great wealth makes rich people "different" from everybody else—in all the wrong ways. Rich people "possess and enjoy early," Fitzgerald said, "and it does something to them, makes them soft where we are hard, and cynical where we are trustful, in a way that, unless you were born rich, it is difficult to understand."[69]

The more thoughtful among the wealthy have sometimes lamented the heavy weight that great wealth places on unwary shoulders. "Observation teaches that, generally speaking, it is not well for the children that they should be so burdened," noted Andrew Carnegie a century ago.[70] But more typical are the men of great wealth who worry more about their fortunes than their children's psyches. "Men who have built up fortunes are often much harder on their offspring than is generally realized," notes journalist William Davis. "Many do not care at all for the idea that their children should be allowed to dissipate the assets they have built up so painstakingly over the years."[71]

Great wealth, philosopher Philip Slater adds, makes wealthy people instinctively suspicious because they're never sure whether they're loved or admired for themselves or for their fortunes. "If you gain fame, power, or wealth, you won't have any trouble finding lovers," Slater notes, "but they will be people who love fame, power, or wealth."[72]

Wealth, Slater points out, also ultimately leaves wealthy people bored with life. Wealth gives the wealthy "too much con-

> *The more thoughtful among the wealthy have sometimes lamented the heavy weight that great wealth places on unwary shoulders.*

trol over what they experience." Rich people "try to translate their own fantasies into reality instead of testing what reality itself has to offer." The endproduct is the elegant stupor that typifies the pace of so many rich people's lives. "When you can control what comes to you in life," Slater notes, "life itself loses most of its excitement."[73]

For similar reasons, wealth often tends to perpetuate infantile behavior.

"Learning and growth are very difficult with wealth," Philip Slater explains, "because they depend on experiences in real life, and wealth enables one to buy out of life."[74]

We non-rich understand all these dynamics. "It is," writes editor Lewis Lapham, "nothing new to say that an inordinate love of money results in predictably high yields of stupidity and despair."[75] Still, wealth remains tempting to us—no matter how many ministers thunder against its corrupting influence. If *we* had the money the wealthy now have, so many of us in the non-rich majority believe, things would be different. *We* would retain our humanity. *We* wouldn't become the poor excuses for well-rounded, caring, compassionate individuals the wealthy so often appear to be. This may be our saddest illusion.

"To suppose, as we all suppose, that we could be rich and not behave the way the rich behave, is like saying that we could drink all day and stay sober," critic L. P. Smith once noted.[76]

"I have known some drunks who were happy at times," adds Philip Slater, "but I've known no one who devoted a long life to alcohol and didn't suffer from it, and I believe the same to be true for wealth."[77]

For Slater, the pursuit of wealth is an addiction, little different from alcoholism or any other drug dependency. Wealth addiction, notes Slater, "deprives us of more nourishing human satisfactions—love, friendship, adventure, physical well-being."[78]

The hunger for ever greater wealth may well be an addiction, but it's an addiction, as Slater recognizes, fostered and nourished by the very structure of modern American economic life. Our society rewards and honors, above all else and above all others, wealth and those who accumulate it. The same 1990 *Fortune* magazine poll that asked Americans how they, personally, measure the success of their lives also asked Americans to identify the main symbol of success in America today. Eighty percent gave a simple answer: money.

This money, others have observed, makes for an empty symbol.

"Money brings some happiness," notes playwright Neil Simon. "But after a certain point it just brings more money."[79]

But money, of course, doesn't just bring "more money." The pursuit of ever greater quantities of money sets a most "disagreeable" moral tone that pits person against person. "We all suffer when we egg each other on to greater grasping," writes Philip Slater, "instead of enjoying the real possibility of shared resources."[80]

To make matters worse, this constant grasping for more, most often by those who already have enough, simply makes no sense.

"What many people are beginning to realize," writes social philosopher Paul Wachtel, "is that now time is more precious than goods, that indeed we hardly have time to consume what we can already afford."[81]

The mad chase for wealth—and the tolerance of the wide disparities in wealth that this chase invariably produces—fosters far more than irrationality. The wealth chase undermines the social

> *To suppose, as we all suppose, that we could be rich and not behave the way the rich behave, is like saying we could drink all day and stay sober.*

solidarity that's essential to any society that aims to be free, open, and caring. A "common culture," British historian R. H. Tawney once wrote, "is incompatible with the existence of sharp contrasts between the economic standards and educational opportunities of different classes, for such contrasts have as their result, not a common culture, but servility or resentment, on the one hand, and patronage or arrogance, on the other."[82] Adds sociologist Jennifer Hochschild: "Unchecked, economic values lead to an unmitigated meritocracy in which the rich are seen as successes and good, and the poor as failures and bad. The devastating effects for both rich and poor are obvious. People refrain from activities with no market value; they blame themselves excessively for poverty and praise themselves excessively for wealth. . ."[83]

In the eyes of some Americans, there's nothing wrong with the "unmitigated meritocracy" Hochschild fears. The problem, these Americans would argue, isn't America's never-ending race for wealth. The problem—the root cause of envy and resentment and social discord—is the baggage that some racers are unfairly asked to carry. If we just made sure that all racers were equally burdened at the starting line, goes this reasoning, the race results would be seen as fair by all. The worthy would be rewarded. Their fellow racers would accept the final standings with equanimity.

This is the rhetoric of "equal opportunity." In modern American life, this rhetoric dominates our political discourse, and ambitious political leaders constantly genuflect before it, for good reason. The rhetoric of equal opportunity offers politicians a good excuse *not* to challenge inequality of income and wealth. Under equal opportunity theory, inequality becomes socially acceptable, as long as everyone has the same chance as everyone else to become more unequally rich.

If life were as straightforward as a road race, equal opportunity might be an adequate guide for social policy. But in life there is no starter's gun, and that reality makes equal opportunity theory a woefully inadequate approach to life, as economist Arthur Okun and many others have pointed out. Equal opportunity, argues Okun, is rooted in the notion of a fair race, where people are even at the starting line. "What's most difficult," says Okun, "is finding the starting line." Asks Okun:

> Does the line begin at differences in prenatal influences? Or at the benefits of better childhood health care, achievement-oriented training, educational attainment, family assistance in job placement, inheritance of physical property?[84]

In short, in a society that tolerates wide disparities in wealth, no starting line assures a fair race. Those who come to the race rich will always have a head start, an unfair advantage.

We are left with the wisdom that careful observers ancient and modern have so clearly understood. If we tolerate the presence of the rich, we let envy and grasping limit what we can be, what we ought to be.

"So long as there are people who have more, others will 'need' more," noted economist Herman Miller a generation ago. "If this is indeed the basis for human behavior, then obviously the gap between the rich and the poor cannot be ignored, however high the *minimum* levels of living may be raised."[85]

"I doubt that we Americans can come to terms with our money neuroses without understanding the more florid pathology of the very rich," concludes Philip Slater, "for it is our envy and admiration of the rich that supports their habit and keeps us hooked ourselves."[86]

In a society that tolerates wide disparities in wealth, there is no starting line that assures a fair race. Those who start the race rich will always have a head start.

Wealth and Inevitability

If the rich are so hazardous to our society's health—so hazardous to our democracy, our economy, our character—then why haven't the rest of us, the vast non-rich majority, "done something"? Why are the rich as rich as ever?

Could it be that rich people are a natural, unavoidable outgrowth of human society? Could it be that all attempts to seriously limit or eliminate great disparities in wealth are, at best, futile exercises?

Or is a rich people-free society still very much a realizable goal? Are past failures to eliminate disparities in wealth merely lessons that future campaigns against wealth must take to heart and learn from?

For some answers to these questions, we need to turn now to the historical record.

Notes

1. Jeffrey G. Williamson and Peter H. Lindert *American Inequality: A Macroeconomic History* (New York: Academic Press, 1980), p. 7.

2. "Trends....In Wealth Distribution," *Economic Notes*, November-December 1986, pp.10-13.

3. Mortimer Lipsky *A Tax on Wealth* (Cranberry, N.J.: A.S. Barnes and Company, 1977), p. 84.

4. Henry Phelps Brown *Egalitarianism and the Generation of Inequality* (Oxford: Clarendon Press, 1988), p.344.

5. Marvin Schwartz and Barry Johnson "Estimates of Personal Wealth 1986," *Statistics of Income Bulletin*, Spring 1990, p.63.

6. "Richest 1.6% in US Hold 28.5% of Wealth," *Boston Globe*, August 23, 1990.

7. Spencer Rich "Gap Found in Wealth Among Races," *The Washington Post*, January 11, 1991, p. A3.

8. David Wessel "Wealth of U.S. Households Stayed Flat After Four Years Despite '80s Expansion," *Wall Street Journal*, January 11, 1991.

9. Arthur M. Okun "Equality of Income and Opportunity" in A.B. Atkinson, ed., *Wealth, Income, and Inequality*, second edition (New York: Oxford University Press, 1980), p. 16.

10. Quoted in Lewis H. Lapham *Money and Class in America* (New York:

11. Edmund Faltermayer "Who Are the Rich?" *Fortune*, December 17, 1990. p. 95.

12. Rich, op.cit., p. A3.

13. Robert Reich "Secession of the Successful," *New York Times Magazine*, January 20, 1991.

14. Frank Lalli "Editor's Notes," *Money*, December, 1990, p.7.

15. Faltermayer, op.cit., p. 96.

16. Lawrence Mishel and David M. Frankel *The State of Working America, 1990-91 Edition* (Washington, D.C.: Economic Policy Institute, 1990), p.25.

17. Robert Greenfield and Scott Barancik From a Center on Budget and Policy Priorities report quoted in *The Washington Post*, July 7, 1990.

See also Robert S. McIntyre *Inequality & the Federal Budget Deficit* (Washington, D.C.: Citizens for Tax Justice, 1991) for statistical estimates that update the income distribution story through 1992.

18. Ibid., p.45.

19. Quoted in Herman P. Miller *Rich Man, Poor Man* (New York: Thomas Y. Crowell Company, 1964), p. 2.

20. See Richard Parker *The Myth of the Middle Class* (New York: Liveright, 1972), p.119.

21. Alan A. Tait *The Taxation of Personal Wealth*

Weidenfeld & Nicolson), p. 22.

(Urbana: University of Illinois Press, 1967), p.10.

22. William Davis *The Rich: A Study of the Species* (New York: Franklin Watts, 1983), p. xv.

23. Ibid., p. 252.

24. Ibid., p. 256.

25. Philip Slater *Wealth Addiction* (New York: E.P. Dutton, 1980), p. 95.

26. Quoted in Miller, *Rich Man, Poor Man*, op. cit., p. 8.

27. Quoted in Randolph E. Paul *Taxation in the United States* (Boston: Little, Brown and Company, 1954), p.125.

28. Ibid., p. 742.

29. Davis, op.cit., p.187.

30. Joseph J. Thorndike, Jr. *The Very Rich: A History of Wealth* (New York: American Heritage/Bonanza Books, 1976), p. 22.

31. Fred Harris "Let's Not Give Up on Democracy: A Normative Approach to Contemporary Democratic Theory," in Mark E. Kann ed., *The Future of American Democracy*, (Philadelphia: Temple University Press, 1983), p. 214.

32. Brown, ibid., p. 71.

33. Richard Parker *The Myth of the Middle Class: Notes on Affluence and Equality* (New York: Liveright, 1972), p. 58-59. Author's paraphrase.

34. J. R. Pole
     The Pursuit of Equality in American History (Berkeley: University of California Press, 1978), p.121.

35. Ibid., p. 122.

36. Quoted in "Wealth Triumphs, We Lose," *In These Times* editorial, August 6-19, 1986.

37. "Campaign Reform," Coalition for Democratic Values, position paper, Silver Spring, Maryland, 1990.

38. Poll by Voter Research and Surveys of New York.

39. Quoted in Parker, op.cit., p. 186.

40. Ravi Batra
     Surviving the Great Depression of 1990 (New York: Simon & Schuster, 1988), p.17.

41. Ravi Batra
     The Great Depression of 1990 (New York: Simon & Schuster, 1987), p.117.

42. Batra, *Surviving the Great Depression of 1990*, op.cit., p. 22

43. Huey P. Long
     Every Man a King: The Autobiography of Huey P. Long (New Orleans: National Book Company, Inc., 1935), p. 298.

44. Batra, *The Great Depression of 1990*, op.cit., p. 120.

45. Ibid., p. 122.

46. Mishel and Frankel, op.cit., p. 2.

47. Ibid., p. 3.

48. Charles Heckscher
     "Can Business Beat Bureauracy?" in *The American Prospect*, Spring 1991, p. 114.

49. Ibid., p. 119.

50. Peter F. Drucker
     The Changing World of the Executive (New York: Times Books, 1982), p. 22.

51. John Kenneth Galbraith
     Economics and the Public Purpose (Boston: Houghton Mifflin Company, 1973), p. 293.

52. Drucker, op.cit., pp. 22-23.

53. Joani Nelson-Horchler
     "What's Your Boss Worth?" *The Washington Post*, August 6, 1990, p. D3.

54. Quoted by Colman McCarthy
     "Do They Deserve a Raise?" *The Washington Post*, December 20, 1986, p. A21.

55. Nelson-Horchler, op.cit., p. D3.

56. Quoted in Lapham, op.cit., p. 230.

57. Warner Woodworth
     "The Scandalous Pay of the Corporate Elite," in *Business and Society Review*, Spring, 1987, p. 22.

58. Ibid., p. 23.

59. Ibid.

60. Paul, op.cit., p. 747.

61. R.M. Hare in John Arthur and William H. Shaw, eds.
     Justice and Economic Distribution (Englewood Cliffs, N.J.: Prentice-Hall, Inc., 1978), p. 126.

62. Leviticus. 25:16.

63. Ecclesiastes. 5:19.

64. Mark. 10:25.

65. Thomas Schmidt
     "The Hard Sayings of Jesus," in David Neff, ed., *The Midas Trap* (Wheaton, Illinois: Victor Books, 1990), p. 21.

66. Ibid., p. 18.

67. Lapham, op.cit., p. 27.

68. Anne B. Fisher
     "A Brewing Revolt Against the Rich," *Fortune*, December 17, 1990, p. 90.

69. Quoted in Davis, op.cit., frontispiece.

70. Andrew Carnegie
     The Gospel of Wealth in Poverty and Wealth (Lynchburg College), p. 377.

71. Davis, op.cit., p. 142.

72. Slater, op.cit., p. 29.

73. Ibid., p. 28.

74. Ibid., p. 30.

75. Lapham, op.cit., p. 213.

76. Quoted in Lapham, ibid., p. 169.

77. Slater, op.cit., p. 28.

78. Ibid., p. 37.

79. Quoted in Slater, ibid., p. 49.

80. Ibid., p. 150.

81. Paul L. Wachtel
     The Poverty of Affluence (Philadelphia: New Society Publishers, 1989), p. 161.

82. R.H. Tawney
     "The Religion of Inequality" in Atkinson, ed., op.cit., p. 8.

83. Jennifer L. Hochschild
     What's Fair?: American Beliefs about Distributive Justice (Cambridge: Harvard University Press, 1981), p. 68.

84. Arthur M. Okun
     "Equality of Income and Opportunity in Wealth, Income, and Inequality" in Atkinson, ed., op.cit., p. 22.

85. Miller, op.cit., p. 39.

86. Slater, op.cit., p. 18.

2. The Wars Against Wealth

Nobody gave Hattie Caraway much of a chance. In the 1932 Arkansas election for United States senator, Caraway, a caretaker incumbent appointed to the seat held by her late husband, faced six other candidates. A week before the election, no one in Arkansas politics considered her a viable contender.[1]

But Hattie Caraway had, in her brief stint as senator, made one very astute move. She had earned the gratitude of the junior senator from Louisiana, Huey P. Long, by supporting his proposed Senate resolution to limit the wealth and incomes of America's richest people.

In the closing weeks of Hattie Caraway's campaign, Long repaid the favor. He brought his tax-the-rich and share-the-wealth message to the Depression-ravaged farmers of Arkansas, all the time singing Hattie Caraway's praises.

"Think of it, my friends!" Long told one cheering rally. "In 1930 there were 540 men in Wall Street who made $100,000,000 more than all the wheat farmers and all the cotton farmers and all the cane farmers of this country put together."

"And you people," the homespun Long added, "wonder why your belly's flat up against your backbone!"[2]

On Election Day, Hattie Caraway pulled a political miracle.

She won her Senate bid, receiving more votes than the other six candidates combined. In 1932, such was the power and the reach of Huey P. Long.

Today, we remember Huey Long, if we remember him at all, as a rustic eccentric, the root of a Louisiana political dynasty, a colorful political clown who never missed a parade, a dark, evil force whose strong-arm tactics as governor helped earned him the label as "the most dangerous man in America."

What's been forgotten is what Huey Long had to say and the political significance of his immense popularity. For a brief few years, Long led the most popular campaign against rich people in American history.

Huey Long, a critical biographer noted years ago, "dared put his fingers into the real ulcer of social evil in American life," the inequitable distribution of wealth.[3] And he spoke a political language Depression America could understand.

"Unless you redistribute the wealth of a country into the hands of the people every fifty years, your country's got to go to ruination," Long warned. "Too many men running things that think they're smarter than the Lord."[4]

Most Americans found Long's analysis of the Depression eminently sensible. "There's too much concentration of wealth among a few people," Long noted in one 1932 interview.[5] "Now as long as the government permits the pilin' up of huge individual fortunes, which is expressly forbidden in *Leviticus*, we are goin' to have crime and spoilin' and trouble," he added in another.[6]

In 1932, on the floor of the United States Senate, Long proposed that the tax laws "be so revamped that no one man should be allowed to have an income of more than one million dollars a year" and that "no one person should inherit in a lifetime more than five million dollars without working for it."[7]

"What is a man going to do with more than $1,000,000?" Long asked his Senate colleagues.[8] "If we could distribute this surplus wealth, while leaving these rich people all the luxuries they can possibly use, what a different world this would be."[9]

Long's resolution received only a handful of Senate votes, but people—and politicians—took notice. In the 1932 Presidential campaign, Franklin Roosevelt and Herbert Hoover both echoed Long's egalitarian message.

FDR, accepting the Democratic nomination, announced that Americans "look to us for guidance and for a more equitable opportunity to share in the distribution of the national wealth."[10] Hoover told a campaign rally in New York's Madison Square Garden that he longed for an America "where wealth is not concentrated in the hands of a few, but diffused among the lives of all."[11]

One month after FDR's election, Long reintroduced his Senate resolution. This time, his proposal to cap wealth and income received 20 yeas.[12]

The "Long Plan" that the senator from Louisiana put before the Senate and the American people was to go through several variations. But the basics always remained constant: a ceiling on the income and wealth of the very rich that would create a floor of decency for everyone else. One early version of the plan proposed a 1 percent tax on all individual wealth between $1 million and $2 million, with that tax rate progressively increasing until it reached 100 percent on all fortunes over $100 million. The effect, said Long, would limit "the size of any one man's fortune to something like $50,000,000" and allow "millionaires to have more than they can use for any luxury they can enjoy on earth."

In 1932, Huey Long's proposal to limit the incomes of America's wealthy received the support of 20 United States senators.

This same Long Plan added a $5 million lifetime limit on inheritances and a $1 million annual income limit.[13]

Long had left the 1932 Democratic convention convinced that Franklin Roosevelt shared his tax-the-rich commitment. But the early New Deal made no significant moves toward redistributing the nation's wealth, and Long soon moved to formalize his movement. Long's "Share-Our-Wealth" campaign, launched in 1934, aimed to guarantee $5,000 to every family and free college for all qualified young people, all financed by a capital levy on the savings of the wealthy.[14]

"In order to cure all of our woes," Long told the nation in a February 1934 radio address, "it is necessary to scale down the big fortunes, that we may scatter the wealth to be shared by all the people."[15]

Huey Long had big plans for his movement. "What would you say," he asked one reporter, "if I had a majority of the voters signed up in every Congressional district in the country only to vote for a Share-Our-Wealth candidate?"[16]

These were not idle musings. By mid-1935, Long's Share-Our-Wealth clubs claimed 7 million members. Even allowing for "considerable exaggeration," noted one critical journalist, this total "represented the largest active political organization ever put together in this country."[17]

In all, Long claimed 27,431 Share-Our-Wealth clubs in 1935.[18] That total, undoubtedly inflated, was real enough to frighten FDR's political strategists. Their secret polling found that Long could pull 3 to 4 million votes if he ran for President in 1936.[19] And the Presidency was clearly what Long was after. In mid-1935, Long busied himself writing a novel later published as *My First Days in the White House*. Those first days of the Long Administration, he left no doubt, would be momentous. After his inauguration, Long wrote, Congress would declare "that it was against the public policy of the United States for any one person to possess wealth in excess of one hundred times the average family fortune."[20]

Huey Long may have been every bit the power-hungry pol that contemporary critics and later historians and dramatists have made him out to be. But the share-the-wealth ethos that Huey Long professed was not some idiosyncratic passion. The Huey Long attack on the inequities of wealth and income distribution capped more than a half-century of American tax-the-rich tumult.

Long himself first caught public attention when, as a young attorney, he defended a Louisiana state senator who had been caught up in that tumult. The state lawmaker, S. J. Harper, had been indicted by a federal grand jury for violating the Espionage Act. Harper's crime? During World War I, he had campaigned for Congress on a platform "calling for the conscription of wealth." Long won Harper's acquital.[21]

The Huey Long attack on the inequities of wealth and income distribution capped more than a half-century of American tax-the-rich tumult.

The Roots of the Tax-the-Rich Tradition

Huey P. Long and S. J. Harper both hailed from Winn Parish, the hotbed of Louisiana's Populist revolt against wealth and privilege in the 1890s. In Winn Parish and throughout the South, the Populist crusade united poor farmers, white and black, in electoral struggles that were eventually crushed by simple violence and fraud. By the late 1890s, the People's Party had been beaten into the political margins, and, in 1900, a Winn Parish man ran one of Populism's last-gasp campaigns. This die-hard standard-bearer was, predictably, routed. How much attention the young

Huey Long paid to the campaign we don't know. But it's likely young Huey imbibed the candidate's Populist message. The candidate was his father.[22]

In its mid-1890s heyday, the Populist message of economic, political, and social equality swept America's South and West. For the Populists, equity meant that the rich had to be cut down to democratic size. Their instrument of choice: a federal income tax.

Today, we take the existence of a federal income tax for granted. For us, the income tax is just another tax burden that all Americans must resentfully bear. For the Populists and like-minded reformers in the 1890s, the income tax was something else again. The income tax was a tax on the rich, the key to redistributing America's wealth.

Ironically, for the Civil War-era lawmakers who enacted the nation's first federal income tax law, redistribution was never a motive. In 1861, the Lincoln Administration needed revenue, in massive amounts, to wage the war against secession. The traditional sources of federal revenue—"custom duties, supplemented by the income from the sale of public lands"[23]—were quickly seen as woefully inadequate. An income tax seemed the best alternative.

The first of the Civil War income tax levies enacted by Congress placed a 3 percent tax on incomes over $800. The 1861 measure drew little controversy. If some Americans were going to give up their lives for the union, the least people with income could do was pay a little tax.[24] The 1861 revenue legislation also included America's first inheritance tax.

"Millionaires like Mr. W. B. Astor, Commodore Vanderbilt," the *New York Herald* approvingly noted, "will henceforth contribute a fair proportion of their wealth to the support of the national government."[25]

No taxes were actually collected under the 1861 measure,[26] and collections didn't actually begin until 1862 when new legislation established a $600 exemption and taxed all income between $600 and $10,000 at 3 percent. Income above $10,000 was taxed slightly higher, at 5 percent.[27]

The new commissioner of internal revenue, working "day and night in a small room in the Treasury building with three clerks borrowed from other departments," was soon pulling in the revenue by the bucket. One cashier with a salary of $1,600 a year collected $37 million worth of income taxes in just six months.[28] But the war was costing $2 million a day, and Congress soon found itself upping the income tax ante. The tax act of 1864 set the rates at 5 percent for income between $600 and $5,000, 7.5 percent between $5,000 and $10,000, and 10 percent over $10,000.[29] The next year, Congressman Lewis W. Ross tried unsuccessfully to raise the top rate to 20 percent on income over $20,000. The Ross effort failed, but the final legislation enacted in 1865 did drop the 10 percent tax threshold down to $5,000.[30]

The war-time willingness to tax the rich ended as soon as the shooting stopped. "As the Civil War faded into memory," historian Sidney Ratner notes, "business interests gradually gathered strength to oppose the income and inheritance taxes which had received such strong support from the people when the Union was at stake."[31] The counterattack against the income tax minced no words. Academic Goldwin Smith denounced the income tax's "socialistic tendency." It was, he charged in 1866, "a tax imposed expressly on the rich, and capable of indefinite expansion and class graduation." The progressive income tax, added Rep. Justin S. Morrill "can only be defended on the same ground the high-

> *For the Populists, equity meant that the rich had to be cut down to democratic size. Their instrument of choice: a federal income tax.*

wayman defends his acts."[32]

The income tax, to be sure, had its defenders. Rep. Austin Blair of Michigan noted that "every dollar which we take off this income tax, which applies to the rich men of the country, must be laid upon the poorer men of the country." Rep. Washington Townsend of Pennsylvania charged that the "clamor in favor of the abolition of the income tax" had been cynically orchestrated by "men of colossal fortunes and extraordinary incomes."[33] In the Senate, John Sherman called the income tax "the only discrimination in our tax laws that will reach wealthy men as against the poorer classes."[34]

Sherman and other income tax advocates were fighting a losing battle. In 1867, Congress eliminated higher tax rates for higher incomes and set a flat income tax rate of 5 percent on all incomes over $1,000.[35] In 1868, 250,000 Americans out of a population of 39.5 million paid income tax.[36] By 1872, the last year before the Civil War income tax died completely, only 72,949 Americans, less than one fifth of 1 percent of the nation's population, were paying any taxes on their incomes.[37]

The 1873 repeal of the income tax gave America's most fortunate few a green light to amass wealth totally unfettered by government limitation. And amass wealth they did. Over the next 30 years, the "Gilded Age," fortunes soared to heights scarcely imaginable only a few years before. The United States had until the Civil War always boasted a relatively even distribution of income, at least compared to aristocratic Europe. "By the early twentieth century," note economists Jeffrey G. Williamson and Peter H. Lindert, "wealth concentration had become as great in the United States as in France or Prussia."[38]

Journalists and scholars of the era tracked this growing concentration. In 1892, the *New York Tribune* raised eyebrows by publishing a list of America's millionaires, all 4,047 of them. The following year, an article by a Census Bureau official revealed that .03 percent of the nation's families—the millionaires—owned 20 percent of the nation's wealth. The next 8.97 percent owned another 51 percent, which meant that the nation's wealthiest 9 percent owned 71 percent of the country's treasure.[39]

A widely discussed 1895 book, *The Present Distribution of Wealth in the United States* by Charles B. Spahr, offered some additional damning numbers. The wealthiest 200,000 families in America, those families with incomes over the then princely sum of $5,000, received 30 percent of national income, noted Spahr. These rich Americans paid taxes of various sorts that amounted to 1 percent of their incomes, at the same time average Americans were paying taxes that cost them 4 percent of their incomes.[40] In the same year Spahr's book appeared, Mrs. William Backhouse Astor, Jr., the scion of New York's greatest fortune, dramatically underscored the human dimension of Spahr's statistics. She built a Fifth Avenue mansion with a ballroom big enough for 1,200 guests.[41]

Wealth's dizzying climb in the Gilded Age did not go unopposed. Between 1873 and 1879, lawmakers from the West and South introduced 14 bills to reenact the income tax.[42] In 1880, Felix Adler, the founder of the Ethical Culture Movement, called for "an income tax graduated up to 100 percent on all income above that needed to supply all the comforts and refinements of life."[43] In 1883, crusading newspaper publisher Joseph Pulitzer made the demand for an income tax part of his New York World's 10-plank platform for social reform.[44] In 1886, the Knights of Labor, what was then American labor's largest national organiza-

> *The 1873 repeal of the Civil War income tax gave America's fortunate few a green light to amass wealth totally unfettered by government limitation.*

tion, announced its support for a graduated income tax.[45] By 1890, the income tax was part and parcel of every significant American social reform agenda.

But the graduated income tax was only the most politically plausible of a number of ideas then circulating to limit wealth and income. In his widely read 1879 book, *Progress and Poverty*, Henry George had attacked the concentration of land ownership and proposed the abolition of all taxes, except those upon land values. This "single tax" on land would expropriate all rental income. George's "single tax" prescription won him enough adherents to run a credible campaign for mayor of New York.[46]

But it was another book, Edward Bellamy's *Looking Backward*, that truly captured America's imagination. Published in 1888, Bellamy's novel told the tale of a nineteenth century Bostonian who awoke a century later to find an America that had conquered inequality. In the new America Bellamy described, all working people earned the same income, but worked different numbers of hours. Workers bid for jobs, and the market set the hours of work required in each job category. If no one bid for a particularly unappetizing job, then the hours required for that job would be reduced until the job became appealing enough to attract bidders. In Bellamy's utopia, workers with unappealing jobs would only have to work a few hours a week.

Bellamy's vision of equality proved immensely popular. In the nineteenth century, only the *Bible* and *Ben-Hur* sold more copies than *Looking Backward*. "Nationalist Clubs" sprung up around the nation to popularize the *Looking Backward* credo. Reformers of every stripe found Bellamy an inspirational force, even if they didn't totally endorse his particular utopian vision. The *Farmers' Alliance*, the paper of the Southern farmers' organization that helped found the Populist movement, offered a free copy of *Looking Backward* with every year's subscription.[47]

Bellamy's inspiration and the election of Populist representatives and senators in 1892 all helped make the income tax once again politically viable. By 1894, Populists and Democrats had coalesced behind legislation that would tax the incomes of the nation's richest 5 percent. Their modest proposal for a 2 percent tax on income above $4,000 struck America's wealthy as absolute madness. "Cries of 'confiscation' were echoed throughout the land," one historian has noted, "to which Populist orators usually replied that these huge incomes were 'stolen' anyway."[48]

The opposition to the 1894 income tax included lawmakers who had supported the income tax 30 years earlier in the feverish flush of Civil War. "In a republic like ours, where all men are equal," Senator John Sherman argued, "this attempt to array the rich against the poor or the poor against the rich is socialism, communism, devilism."[49] Other opponents charged that the income tax would lower wages, dampen incentive, and generate fraud and corruption.[50] The income tax, they noted, would take from the "thrifty and enterprising" and give to the "shiftless and sluggard."[51]

Income tax advocates shrugged off the opposition's heated rhetoric. They had the votes. Their income tax proposal passed as an amendment to the 1894 tariff bill, legislation they knew that President Grover Cleveland, an income tax opponent, couldn't afford to veto. The Democratic hen, the *New York Tribune* noted, had "hatched a Populist chicken at last."[52] On August 28, 1894, the nation—for the first time since the Civil War era—had an income tax.

But not for long. Income tax opponents almost immediately

> In the nineteenth century, only the *Bible* and *Ben-Hur* sold more copies than *Looking Backward*, a novel about an America that had eliminated income inequality.

began plotting a court challenge. They counted on the Supreme Court to "stand like a rock against a 'wave of socialist revolution.'"[53] They were not to be disappointed. On May 20, 1895, less than a year after the income tax became law, a 5-4 Supreme Court majority invalidated the entire 1894 income tax. "The wave of socialistic revolution has gone far," applauded the *New York Sun*, "but it breaks at the foot of the ultimate bulwark set up for the protection of our liberties. Five to four the Court stands like a rock."[54] Dissenting Justice Brown felt the weight of that rock. He hoped the decision might not "prove the first step toward the submergence of the liberties of the people in a sordid despotism of wealth."[55]

The Supreme Court's 1895 ruling, just as Justice Brown feared, did prove a significant step toward a new American politics sculpted by the power of great wealth. In 1896, the Republican Party outspent the Democratic-Populist coalition into oblivion. The GOP expended somewhere between $3.5 and $7 million on the 1896 campaign, an unheard of sum. The funds came from the plutocracy that so worried Justice Brown: $250,000 from Standard Oil, $250,000 from J. P. Morgan, and on and on. The Democrats spent $600,000.[56]

With the Populist-Democratic coalition in tatters, wealth had successfully shoved the income tax off the national political stage. In 1898, no one in Congress seriously proposed an income tax when the Spanish-American War generated demands for new revenue sources. Instead, Congress adopted a weak tax on inheritances, mainly because conservatives, as one historian has noted, "felt that a concession on the inheritance tax was far less of a danger to the wealthy classes than one on the income tax."[57] The 1898 inheritance tax adopted by Congress applied only to those bequests over $1 million left to distant relatives or private bodies.[58] But even this modest attempt to limit wealth couldn't outlast the war. In 1902, the war inheritance tax was repealed.

Enter the Modern Era

By the turn of the century, conservatives had crushed the income tax and the Populist reformers who had championed it. But the dizzying concentration of wealth that had so outraged reformers was still spiraling out of control—and wreaking social havoc. The more sensitive conservatives now saw a socialist movement taking shape, a political movement, as Teddy Roosevelt put it, "far more ominous than any Populist or similar movement of the past." As President, Theodore Roosevelt began fulminating, first softly, then louder, against the malefactors of great wealth. In 1906, Roosevelt called for a "progressive tax on all fortunes beyond a certain amount either given in life or devised or bequested upon death to any individual." Later that same year, he cautiously promoted the idea of an income tax. "The man of great wealth," said Roosevelt, "owes a peculiar obligation to the state because he derives special advantages from the mere existence of government." By 1907, Roosevelt was advocating new taxes on income and wealth because "most great civilized countries have an income tax and an inheritance tax."[59]

Roosevelt was playing to the public sentiment, growing once again, that great wealth ought to be checked. He wasn't particularly perceptive. By the 1909 inauguration of William Howard Taft, almost all leading politicos had realized that overt opposition to taxing the rich would be suicidal. In the 1909 congressional session, after Democrats attached an income tax amendment to

In 1895, the Supreme Court ruled an income tax on the wealthy unconstitutional. In the 1896 Presidential race, the wealthy promptly outspent their opposition into oblivion.

a tariff bill, GOP leaders quickly came up with an income tax proposal of their own. President Taft and Senate Finance Committee Chairman Nelson Aldrich proposed, as an alternative to the Democratic legislation, a constitutional amendment that would expressly allow Congress to levy an income tax. The GOP duo also backed an excise tax on corporations, the first tax on corporate profits since the Civil War.

"By supporting the corporation tax and the constitutional amendment," writes historian Sidney Ratner, the GOP old guard leaders "could pose in the 1910 election campaigns as spokesmen for the common people."[60] Taft's proposal to add an income tax amendment to the Constitution passed the Senate 77-0 and the House 318-14. But his careful plan then started to unravel. State legislatures actually started *ratifying* the proposed constitutional amendment enacted by Congress, instead of letting the amendment die the quiet death that the GOP old guard had expected. John D. Rockefeller was aghast. The unthinkable—an income tax on the rich—could become reality. Rockefeller rushed to mobilize opposition to the income tax ratification drive. "When a man has accumulated a sum of money within the law, that it to say, in the legally correct way," pronounced Rockefeller, "the people no longer have any right to share in the earnings resulting from the accumulation."[61]

By 1913, enough states had ignored Rockefeller to make the income tax the 16th amendment to the Constitution. Woodrow Wilson, meanwhile, had been elected President in 1912, and the stage was set for the passage of income tax legislation that would take advantage of the new constitutional taxing authority. In 1913, an income tax finally passed Congress.

The new income tax fell solely on the nation's wealthiest 2 percent of the population, but not very hard. The slightly graduated rates in the 1913 legislation ranged from 1 percent on income between $4,000 and $20,000 to 7 percent on income above $500,000.[62] The same Congress that enacted the modest 1913 income tax defeated a more ambitious proposal from Senator George Norris that would have placed a 75 percent tax on inheritances.[63]

Inequality in America, little changed since the robber baron days that so angered the Populist generation, was safe. Researchers reported that 44 American families were pulling in more than $50 million a year just before World War I—at the same time the majority of adult workers were earning between $10 and $20 a week.[64]

This gaping inequality, U.S. Industrial Relations Commission Research Director Basil M. Manly told Congress in 1915, was a major cause of the unrest then shaking American industry.[65] Manly asked Congress to limit inheritances from any estate to $1 million,[66] and, in 1916, Congress did enact the nation's first permanent estate tax.[67] But the impetus for the legislation was the war in Europe, not any outrage over inequality. The federal income tax, meanwhile, remained "little more than a nuisance to the well-off,"[68] even after 1916 legislation raised the maximum "surtax" on large incomes from 6 to 13 percent.[69]

America's actual entrance into the war in 1917 changed everything. Once again, war's insatiable thirst for revenue drove lawmakers to contemplate tax rates on the wealthy that would have been unthinkable in peace-time. Congressman Keating of Chicago, for instance, proposed a tax bill amendment that would have imposed a 96 percent "surtax" on incomes over $150,000, on top of a 4 percent normal tax.[70]

> *In 1917, war's insatiable thirst for revenue drove lawmakers to contemplate tax rates on the wealthy that would have been unthinkable in peace-time.*

"The effect of the new section will be to tax all incomes above $150,000 100 percent," Keating explained on the floor of Congress. "A man who had an income of $150,000 would be taxed 33 1/3 percent and he would have left a net income of $100,000, but no one in the Republic would have an income in excess of $100,000."

This income limit, Keating added, would raise between $1.6 and $1.7 billion "without oppressing any man, without laying an unreasonable burden upon any industry."[71] To arguments that his income cap would discourage millionaires from making investments, Keating was unapologetic.

"Well, my friend, if you pass my amendment, we will take the millionaire's money, we will take his excess profits, and we will invest it," argued Congressman Keating. "Uncle Sam is not going to put this money in a strong box and permit it to remain there. Uncle Sam will take it and invest it in those things necessary in order to maintain an army in the field. If you adopt my amendment, it will not be necessary for you to enact further bond bills or to appeal to millionaires to purchase bonds. The object of this amendment is to take the excess profits and the excess incomes from the rich of this country and use that money to pay the running expenses of the Government."[72]

Keating was no isolated crackpot. In 1917, an American Committee on War Finance was busily and somewhat successfully beating the bushes mobilizing public support for a "conscription of wealth." The committee called for a 98 percent surtax on incomes over $100,000, which, when added to the 2 percent normal tax enacted in 1916, would have taxed away all incomes over $100,000.[73] Committee heavyweights ranged from millionaire Amos Pinchot, who testified on the committee's behalf before Congress, to newspaper magnate E. W. Scripps, who wired President

Wilson his support for taxing all incomes above $50,000 "for the support of the Government."[74]

The American Committee on War Finance took ads in major newspapers to advocate its income cap proposal and claimed endorsements from organizations representing millions of Americans. These organizations, Amos Pinchot noted in his Senate testimony, "have expressed the belief that the war can not be either justly or efficiently carried on unless people who do not fight but have plenty of money are made to realize their responsibility and forced to give to the Government the use of their wealth, at least to the extent of a heavy tax on large incomes."[75]

The income limits advanced by Pinchot's committee and Congressman Keating didn't pass, but they did help create a climate of opinion that encouraged Congress to escalate the top tax rates on America's richest taxpayers. The 1917 War Revenue Act placed a 50 percent surtax on incomes over 1 million.[76] In 1917, Congress also raised the top estate tax rates up to 25 percent[77] and enacted the nation's first excess profits tax on corporations.[78] A year later, the 1918 Revenue Act upped the total maximum tax rate on high incomes to 77 percent.[79]

Few wealthy Americans actually ended up paying taxes at that substantial rate, but the high tax rates of the World War I era definitely did have bite. Between 1917 and 1919, less than 1 percent of the tax returns Americans filed reported incomes over $20,000. Yet this elite group paid 70 percent of the nation's total income tax revenues.[80]

In war time, with conscripted Americans sacrificing their lives, wealthy Americans felt they had no choice but to grin and bear the indignity of high taxes. But once the war ended in Europe, the wealthy opened a new battlefront in the United

During World War I, a broad-based public campaign asked Congress to tax away all incomes over $100,000. One newspaper magnate wanted the maximum income set at $50,000.

States, against high taxes. Their champion was Andrew Mellon, the multi-millionaire who became the Secretary of the Treasury for the newly elected President, Warren G. Harding.

Mellon, treasury secretary throughout the 1920s, guided one tax cut after another into law. Between 1918 and 1926, the top tax rate on high incomes fell from 77 to 25 percent.[81] Once again, as had happened after the Civil War, the dismantling of a wartime tax structure set the stage for a vast new concentration of wealth in the hands of America's most fortunate few. By 1929, wealth was more unevenly distributed than at any time in recorded American history.

But the nation's economic bubble burst the very same year, and, as the country sank into depression, reformers counterattacked. From Louisiana, Huey Long began his march into national prominence. But the outrage Long articulated wasn't limited to any one section of the country. Reformers of every stripe made inequality the key culprit for "the Depression."

"The whole thing has collapsed," noted New York Congressman Fiorello LaGuardia in 1932, "and there will be nothing left unless we provide an economic readjustment, a better distribution, and that we can do by breaking up those fortunes."[82]

The Revenue Act of 1932 started the work of undoing the damage wrought by the 1920s giveaway to the wealthy. The legislation upped the maximum surtax on high incomes to 55 percent, making the combined top rate on high incomes 63 percent.[83] But many members of Congress felt that the legislation didn't go nearly far enough.

"It is a crime to have millions of people starving and hungry while a few others, who neither toil nor do they spin, are living in luxury," charged the Republican progressive, Senator George

Norris of Nebraska.[84]

America could only fight its way out of the Depression, others argued, if the wealthy subsidized relief programs for the impoverished majority. Senator Lafollette of Wisconsin promised in 1933 "to fight for increased inheritance and income taxes—the likes of which we have never heard of—so that those with huge incomes will have to cough up to help pay for [the federal relief] program."[85]

On the House of Representatives side, Congressman Wesley Lloyd of Washington State introduced a resolution that called for a constitutional amendment that would empower Congress to limit annual incomes to $1 million.

"There is no thinking man in our Nation but who knows that the only reason there is widespread poverty is that wealth and the ownership of wealth has become centralized—the only reason men are too poor is because a few men are too rich," Lloyd told his congressional colleagues. "I propose in the main to bring up the poor and bring down the rich into the class of the average man, where all may find real happiness and where we may know a widespread national prosperity."[86]

Lloyd acknowledged that his maximum income proposal would be an unprecedented step to take.

"I am not insensible [sic] to the fact that this portends a radical departure from preconceived concepts of the rights of property," the Tacoma congressman noted, "but I recognize that a condition has grown upon us that the founders of this Government could not have foreseen." Concluded Lloyd: "Unusual times may demand unusual measures."[87]

By 1935, the height of Huey Long's Share-Our-Wealth movement, tax-the-rich sentiment was everywhere. "It did not require

> *Calls for a cap on the income of the wealthy resurfaced during the Depression. Argued one congressman: 'the only reason men are too poor is because a few men are too rich.'*

much deep thinking for the average person to deduct that there must be something drastically wrong when people are starving in the midst of plenty." noted Minnesota Governor Floyd B. Olson.[88] "If these fortunes are not broken up by law," a distraught Senator Norris confided in a private letter, "the time will come when they will be broken up by the mob."[89]

President Franklin D. Roosevelt, who paid scant attention to tax questions in the early New Deal years, finally had to move. The popular uproar—and the crying need for revenue to finance New Deal programs—had simply become too overwhelming. In his 1935 tax message, the President acknowledged that revenue laws had operated to the "unfair advantage of the few" and "done little to prevent an unjust concentration of wealth and economic power."[90]

"The transmission from generation to generation of vast fortunes by will, inheritance, or gift," said Roosevelt, "is not consistent with the ideals of the American people."[91]

The tax act that finally emerged from Congress in 1935 upped the top rate to 75 percent on incomes over $500,000.[92] But congressional progressives considered that boost a major disappointment. "As finally passed," many felt, "the Wealth Tax Act of 1935 did little either to redistribute wealth or to raise revenue."[93]

The nation's top cheerleader for taxing the wealthy, in the meantime, could do nothing to mobilize the public for more exacting measures. On September 8, 1935, Huey Long was assassinated in Baton Rouge, one day after he boasted that "the passage of [Share-Our-Wealth] laws is the only way they can keep me from being President—unless I die."[94] Long's sudden death, notes one historian, "destroyed the Share-Our-Wealth movement's chances of sweeping northward in 1936."[95]

After Long's assassination, no politically serious popular attempt to up taxes on the wealthy surfaced for the rest of the 1930s. It took a new war, as the decade ended, to force the nation to confront the appalling inequality of wealth and income that Depression-era politics had failed to address.

How deep was that failure? One study of national incomes in mid-Depression found that 41 percent of America's families annually earned less than $1,000 and 87 percent less than $2,500. At the other end of the scale, only 0.97 percent of America's families—270,000 households—took in more than $10,000. Figures from later in the Depression, 1939, demonstrated that families earning under $500—a median income of $346—were paying 22 percent of their income in local, state, and national taxes while families making over $20,000—mean income: $47,000—were paying total taxes at a 37.8 percent rate.[96] Despite a decade of tumult, the Depression 1930s ended as they had begun, with vast disparities of wealth and income. The wealthy, under fierce rhetorical attack throughout the 1930s, had essentially lost very little ground.

> *The Depression 1930s ended as they had begun, with vast disparities of wealth and income. The wealthy had lost very little ground.*

The Rise and Fall of Taxes on the Wealthy

World War II gave New Dealers another chance to make good on their redistributive rhetoric. In the heat of war, the Roosevelt Administration seemed to relish the opportunity.

"Not a single war millionaire will be created in this country as a result of the war disaster," FDR flatly pledged in 1940,[97] and that pledge was soon followed by a series of tax proposals unmatched in American history.

Roosevelt's Secretary of the Treasury, Henry Morgenthau, Jr., dropped the first bombshell by advocating "that all corporate profits over 6 percent on invested capital be taxed away by the government for the period of the emergency."[98]

Morgenthau may have picked up that idea from a 1936 article on war financing published by the American Academy of Political and Social Science. The author, John T. Flynn, had urged an excess profits tax at 6 percent, just what Morgenthau proposed. Flynn's article also proposed new income tax rates that would not permit "the topmost tax-free incomes to exceed $10,000."[99]

This proposal for an income ceiling also became part and parcel of Roosevelt Administration policy. In April 1942, the President announced "that in time of this grave national danger, when all excess income should go to win the war, no American citizen ought to have a net income, after he has paid his taxes, of more than $25,000 a year."[100]

The Treasury Department subsequently fleshed out FDR's proposal in testimony before the House Ways and Means Committee. If FDR's "100 percent war supertax" were enacted, single persons whose before-tax income was $40,000 would be left with $25,000 after the standard tax rates had been applied. Any dollar of income above the $40,000 would be taxed away. For married couples, the 100 percent supertax would kick in on all income over $110,000.[101]

Roosevelt's call for an income ceiling came, predictably, under immediate attack. The *New York Herald Tribune* quickly labeled the $25,000 limit "a blatant piece of demagoguery,"[102] and the House Ways and Means Committee never gave the 100 percent supertax any serious attention. On the House floor, Roosevelt supporters did try to resurrect the maximum income concept. Rep. Adolph Sabath of Illinois proposed a $50,000 individual annual income limit, but Sabath's cap went nowhere.[103]

Roosevelt was not to be deterred. Shortly after Labor Day, FDR repeated his call for $25,000 maximum income, "the only practical way of preventing the incomes and profits of individuals and corporations from getting too high."[104] Congress once again ignored the President's 100 percent supertax, but the Revenue Act of 1942 enacted by Congress did raise the rates on America's wealthiest taxpayers to all-time record levels. The top surtax rate, which had been raised to 77 percent in 1941, jumped to 82 percent. High incomes were also subject to a 6 percent normal tax and a new 5 percent "Victory Tax," which produced a "total marginal rate of 93 percent" on all income over $200,000.[105]

The Victory Tax applied to all Americans with gross incomes over $624,[106] a move that made the income tax a mass tax for the first time in American history. All Americans earning over $12 a week now had income tax withheld from their paychecks,[107] and the proportion of Americans paying federal income taxes soared from 7.1 percent at the start of the war to 64.1 percent by the end.[108]

But the new taxes on both the wealthy and average Americans came nowhere close to meeting the war's insatiable appetite for revenue. In fiscal 1943, the government still had to borrow $60 billion.[109] In response, Congress in 1944 upped the tax rate on the wealthy still again. The new rate schedule placed a 94 percent top rate on all income over $200,000, a rate that significantly exceeded the highest rates in effect during World War I (77 percent on incomes over $1 million) and the Depression (81 percent on incomes over $5 million).[110] The years 1944 and 1945, concludes historian John Witte, "were the most progressive tax years in U.S. history."[111] The World War II tax rate hikes accomplished just

In April 1942, President Franklin Roosevelt proposed that 'no American citizen ought to have a net income, after he has paid his taxes, of more than $25,000 a year.'

what they were intended to do. Government receipts in 1945 were 8.8 times greater than 1939 receipts.[112]

But the war, by 1945, was ending, and the wealthy and their political allies soon joined for the traditional, post-war cut-taxes offensive, this time armed with some new ammunition. With income taxes now levied on broad swatches of the American people, conservatives could justify their across-the-board rate cut proposals as badly needed tax relief for working Americans.

This concern for working people struck congressional liberals as something less than deeply felt. Congressman H. Carl Anderson of Minnesota could see no justification whatsoever for a 3 percent across-the-board tax cut proposal pending before the House Ways and Means Committee. To give $45 in tax relief to a $2,000 a year man, Anderson asked, why must Congress give a millionaire tax relief totaling $90,000, exactly the sum millionaires would save if the 3 percent across-the-board tax cut were enacted?[113] Anderson and his friends were swimming against the tide. The 1945 tax bill enacted by Congress cut the surtax rate 3 percent in each bracket, and, once the war ended, the GOP attack on World War II tax rates escalated.

"For years we Republicans have been warning that the short-haired women and long-haired men of alien minds in the administrative branch of government were trying to wreck the American way of life and install a hybrid oligarchy at Washington through confiscatory taxation," exhorted the new Republican chair of the House Ways and Means Committee, Harold Knutson of Minnesota.[114]

High tax rates, a more sober critic charged, strike "directly at the country's managerial brains."[115] High rates, he explained, were making it difficult for industry to hire good men.

In 1947, the Republican-controlled House of Representatives made cutting tax rates its top order of business. HR 1, the first piece of legislation introduced in the 1947 session, sought to drop the maximum tax rate on high incomes from 85.5 to 76.5 percent. That drop would have meant $164,760 in tax relief to a couple making $500,000 a year.[116] The GOP bill, Congressman Aime Forand of Rhode Island charged, would increase the take-home pay of the 1,401 taxpayers earning over $300,000 by 60 percent. The 46 million taxpayers earning under $5,000, meanwhile, would see a mere 5 percent tax reduction. The Republican tax cut, Forand lamented, would be "the first step in the move to shift the burden of taxation from the backs of the big taxpayers to the backs of the little people." President Harry Truman agreed. He vetoed the 1947 tax cut that emerged from Congress.

The next January, Truman proposed his own version of tax relief. The President's tax cuts would go only to those earning under $5,000, and the loss in federal revenue from the cut would be made up by an excess profits tax.[118] Congress chose to go a different route. The Revenue Act of 1948, enacted over Truman's veto, cut the maximum effective tax rate to 77 percent.[119] That cut wasn't nearly as deep as some powerful Americans had sought. In testimony before Congress, General Motors Chairman Alfred P. Sloan, Jr. had urged a 50 percent top limit. "Excessive or confiscatory taxes as levied on the individual," complained Sloan, "reduce savings for investment and discourage the sacrifice necessary to induce savings."[120]

The outbreak of the Korean War in 1950 put the brakes on the tax cut momentum. Truman quickly sought to undo the cutbacks of 1945 and 1948, and Congress, now in war-time mode, obliged. The 1950 tax bill upped the top bracket tax rate from 82.1 to 91

The years 1944 and 1945 'were the most progressive tax years in U.S. history.' The tax schedule of those years placed a 94 percent top rate on all income over $200,000.

percent and raised the maximum effective rate from 77 to 87 percent.[121] In 1951, the maximum effective rate inched up to 88 percent, which theoretically left a taxpayer netting $500,000 in
income $75,000 in pocket after taxes.[122]

The tax hikes of the early 1950s proved to be the last congressional swipe at the incomes of the wealthy. Throughout the rest
of the decade, a time of heated Cold War, the tax rates held—at
least on paper. In reality, tax avoidance as an art form grew steadily more sophisticated throughout the Eisenhower Administration. Even more significant was the change in political climate.
The old anger against bloated fortunes seemed to disappear as
the 1950s unfolded. By 1961 and the birth of John F. Kennedy's
New Frontier, tax-driven redistribution was nowhere to be seen
on the political agenda.

The new Kennedy Administration, arguing that tax reductions would stimulate economic growth, quickly proposed cutting
the top tax rate from 91 to 65 percent.[123] Economic growth, liberals
of the Kennedy-Johnson years believed, was the quickest route to
social justice. Economic growth would raise the poor from poverty, and ending poverty, not attacking wealth, became the crusading mission of 1960s liberals. Taxes, to be sure, did have a role in
this crusade, but an entirely new role that wouldn't endanger the
incomes of rich people. Instead of taxing the rich, liberals argued,
Congress needed to enact a "negative income tax" to help the poor.

The idea was simple. Federal tax exemptions "should be
raised immediately to a level which would guarantee an untaxed
income adequate for minimum subsistence." Americans below
this income would then be "entitled to receive federal government
payments sufficient to raise their incomes to this level." In one
plan advanced by Robert Theobold, every adult would be guaran-

teed $1,000 a year, with $600 for every child.[124]

The negative income tax idea appeared equally enticing in some conservative circles. In 1969, the Nixon Administration proposed replacing the federal welfare system with a "Family Assistance Plan."[125] Nixon's FAP would have guaranteed a family of four $1,600. A family would be allowed to earn $60 per month above that total tax-free. Income above that $60 figure would cost the poor family $1 in aid for every $2 of wage.

Nixon's FAP proposal eventually stalled and died. Democrats sought a higher income guarantee for the poor, and not many Republicans were ever enthusiastic about FAP to begin with.

George McGovern, Nixon's opponent in the 1972 election, had no better luck with his attempt to guarantee the poor an income via a negative income tax. During the 1972 Presidential primaries, McGovern proposed giving every American an income tax credit of $1,000. The idea: give everyone a tax credit that "would be paid in cash to those persons whose credit exceeded their tax bills."[126] McGovern's proposal proved a major campaign embarrassment. His primary foe, Hubert Humphrey, ridiculed the idea, and "even potential beneficiaries" came to perceive the McGovern plan "only as a new and higher dole to welfare recipients for which they would bear the cost."[127]

The McGovern debacle essentially quashed any serious liberal effort to redistribute income from the bottom up. Middle-income taxpayers, facing higher tax rates each year as inflation pushed them up into higher tax brackets, would have no part of negative income tax proposals. And why should they? At a time when loopholes and government tax rate cuts meant that the rich were paying less in taxes, middle-income people felt that any income guarantee for the poor would come at their expense. By trying to

The tax hikes of the early 1950s, enacted in the heat of the Korean War, proved to be the last congressional swipe at the incomes of the wealthy.

help the poor, without attacking the rich, the liberals of the 1960s and 1970s only exacerbated tensions between middle- and low-income Americans.

By the end of the 1970s, the push against poverty had exhausted itself.[128] The social justice impulse had lost any political relevance. The time was ripe for a conservative counterattack against the tax-code remnants of earlier tax-the-rich fervor, and attack the conservatives did. The counterattack they began in the late 1970s adopted almost whole the tax-cut ideology propagated by Secretary of the Treasury Mellon a half-century earlier.

"By recreating the incentive to work, save, invest and take economic risks, by reducing the percentage of reward for that economic activity taken by the federal government in the form of taxes," noted Rep. Jack Kemp in 1978, "we will have more investment and more risk taking. That will expand the total economic activity, expanding the tax base from which federal tax revenues are drawn, providing additional revenue with which to offset federal budget deficits."[129]

Kemp's tax-cut prescription was essentially enacted into law as the Economic Recovery Tax Act of 1981, the "largest tax cut in history for both individuals and corporations."[130] The 1981 Tax Act reduced income taxes by 23 percent across the board, fixing a top rate on ordinary income of 50 percent.

"This proposal for equal reduction in everyone's tax rates," assured President Ronald Reagan, "will expand our national prosperity, enlarge national income and increase opportunity for all Americans."[131]

The real goal of the Reagan tax cut revolution, Reagan budget official David Stockman was later to reveal, had little to do with providing tax relief for average Americans. "The hard part of the supply-side tax cut is dropping the top rate from 70 to 50 percent," Stockman explained. "In order to make this palatable as a political matter, you had to bring down all the brackets." The 1981 across-the-board tax cut, summed up Stockman, "was always a Trojan Horse to bring down the top rate."[132]

Five years after the tax cut, Congress all but abandoned the principle of progressive taxation. The 1986 tax act did make capital gains taxable at the same rate as ordinary income for the first time since 1921, a long-overdue move that ended the privileged tax status of profits made by buying and selling stocks, bonds, and property. But the 1986 measure also dropped the tax rate on America's highest incomes down to 28 percent, where it remained until 1990 when, after a flurry of tax-the-rich rhetoric just before Election Day, Congress shoved the top rate to 31 percent.[133]

Ronald Reagan's 1981 across-the-board tax cut—'a Trojan Horse' to bring down the top rate on the wealthy—meant little tax relief for average Americans.

The Lessons of the Past

What can we learn from this survey of America's tax-the-rich history? For some historians, any chronicle of American tax history demonstrates the inherent inadequacy of the federal income tax as a vehicle for narrowing disparities in wealth and income.

"What does seem apparent," writes John Witte, "is that legislated tax reduction and reduced progressivity are the historical norm, breaking down only in periods of crisis."[134] The very complexity of the income tax system, says Witte, has undermined its effectiveness as a redistributive mechanism.

"As the income tax grew in scope and complexity," Witte argues, "the larger issues of redistribution and class confrontation were lost in the details of legislative battles."[135]

Witte's point seems unassailable. Today, few Americans see

Table 1
THE TAX BITE ON MILLION-DOLLAR INCOMES

This table tracks how Americans with million-dollar incomes have fared on their federal income taxes. Listed here, for each year, are the number of taxpayers with at least $1 million in income (in 1986 dollars), their mean income, and the tax they paid on this income. The table also compares the share of the nation's income held by millionaires before and after taxes. The final column lists the tax rate for taxpayers making $1 million or more.

Year	Number	Before tax mean income	Average income tax	Pre-tax share	Post-tax share	Average tax rate
1918	2,522	$2,195,723	$1,134,894	8.43	4.60	51.69
1926	4,310	2,485,894	405,981	11.19	9.82	16.33
1935	1,711	2,185,697	990,552	5.20	3.06	45.32
1943	2,673	1,887,594	1,470,976	3.09	0.97	77.93
1951	3,235	1,887,594	1,146.577	2.14	1.11	58.64
1962	3,361	2,198,673	958,313	1.01	0.68	43.59
1975	4,585	2,051,917	932,889	0.69	0.45	45.46
1986	31,859	2,277,695	915,563	4.06	2.94	40.20

Sources: Fritz Scheuren and Janet McCubbin, "Individual Income Tax Shares and Average Tax Rates, 1916-1950," *Statistics of Income Bulletin,* Winter 1988-89, p. 63; and Janet McCubbin and Fritz Scheuren, "Individual Income Tax Shares and Average Tax Rates, 1951-1986," *Statistics of Income Bulletin,* Spring 1989, p. 67.

the federal income tax as the egalitarian instrument that reformers of earlier generations so prized. The income tax appears instead as a heavy weight on working people's shoulders, an inconvenience that rich people somehow always manage to avoid. The U.S. tax system, two top tax experts concluded even before the Reagan era, has "little effect on the distribution of income":

> The very rich pay higher average effective rates than does the average family, but the difference is large only if the corporation income and property taxes are assumed to be borne by capital. If they are assumed to be shifted to consumers to a considerable degree, the very rich pay tax rates that are only moderately higher than average.[136]

Today, few Americans see the federal income tax as the egalitarian instrument that reformers of earlier generations so prized.

The income tax "as a fundamental and ostensibly equitable means of raising revenue has been slowly but continuously eroded," concludes historian Witte. "In the process, any possibility of using the tax system to redistribute income—now or, I believe, in the future—has been lost."[137]

As the 1980s ended, some reformers began looking for other redistributive tools. Some began championing a federal "wealth tax" as an alternative to the income tax. An 8 percent tax applied to all individual wealth over $300,000, argued DePaul University economist William M. Dugger, would have raised $155 billion in 1988, enough to cover that year's entire federal budget deficit.[138]

"In America, everything except wealth is taxed today," noted economist Ravi Batra. "Just because wealth is mainly in the hands of the rich and powerful, there is no reason for it to escape taxation, while production, sales and income are all taxed."[139]

Wealth taxes were a key goal of many British Labor Party activists in the 1970s, and the idea of a wealth tax—a direct tax imposed on the total worth of each individual on a net basis, minus all outstanding liabilities[140]—has always had adherents in the United States. These advocates have argued that wealth is a better measure of economic well-being than income.

"A works as a typist and receives a salary of $5,500 a year," as one wealth tax advocate has put it. "B has deposited $100,000 in a savings bank and receives $5,500 a year in interest. Who has a greater capacity to pay taxes?"[141]

But, as many tax reformers have noted over the years, wealth is hard to measure and even harder to tax. Instituting a wealth tax would require a vast new administrative network. And even with that network in place, many difficult administrative problems would remain, ranging from the technical—matching bearer bonds with their rightful owners—to the deeply philosophical.[142] How, for instance, would assets be valued if a wealth tax were in effect? At their cost? Their fair market value? Their assessed value?[143]

But the real problem with any wealth tax goes deeper. The prospect of a tax on wealth offers little direct relief to the average, non-wealthy taxpayer. Tax-the-rich campaigns, of course, can only succeed by exciting the average, non-wealthy taxpayer. If average taxpayers aren't excited enough to mobilize behind a tax-the-rich effort, there's simply no hope of breaking the grip the wealthy hold on our society, on any society. Historically, tax-the-rich advocates have seldom created this needed excitement, largely because they've seldom drawn the link between higher taxes on the wealthy and improved lives for everyone else.

The predictable result? We as a nation have done virtually nothing to narrow our incredibly wide disparities in wealth and income. Our only steps toward greater equality have come during war time, when politically astute wealthy people have realized they can't ask working people to sacrifice their lives unless they themselves are willing to sacrifice at least a bit of their treasure.

If we as a nation are to solve our rich people problem, then clearly we either need to poke around for some new wars to fight or come up with a new approach to taxing wealthy people that can indeed excite the great majority of Americans. Let's pass on wars. An alternative does exist.

Notes

1. Carleton Beals
The Story of Huey P. Long (Westport: Greenwood Press, 1935, 1971), p. 247.

2. Ibid., p. 244.

3. Ibid., p. 26.

4. Ibid., p. 245.

5. Forrest Davis
Huey Long: A Candid Biography (New York: Dodge Publishing Company, 1935), p. 150.

6. Ibid., p. 155.

7. Huey P. Long
Every Man a King: The Autobiography of Huey P. Long (New Orleans: National Book Co. Inc., 1933), p. 295.

8. Beals, op.cit., p. 230.

9. Long, *Every Man a King*, op.cit., p. 294.

10. Davis, op.cit., p. 299.

11. Long, *Every Man a King*, op.cit., p. 316.

12. Davis, op.cit., p. 174.

13. Long, *Every Man a King*, op.cit., pp. 338-9.

14. David H. Bennett
Demagogues in the Depression (New Brunswick, New Jersey: Rutgers University Press, 1969), pp. 120-1.

15. Huey P. Long
Share Our Wealth: Every Man a King (Washington, D.C.: 1935), p. 7.

16. Davis, op.cit., p. 41.

17. Beals, op.cit., p. 292.

18. Bennett, op.cit., p. 125.

19. Ibid., p. 127.

20. Huey Pierce Long
My First Days in the White House (Harrisburg: The Telegraph Press, 1935), p. 143.

21. Davis, op.cit., p. 71.

22. Lawrence Goodwyn
Democratic Promise: The Populist Moment in America (New York: Oxford University Press, 1976), p. 337.

23. Sidney Ratner
American Taxation: Its History as a Social Force in Democracy (New York: W.W. Norton & Company, Inc., 1942), p. 35.

24. John F. Witte
The Politics and Development of the Federal Income Tax (Madison: The University of Wisconsin Press, 1985), p. 68.

25. Ratner, op.cit., p. 67.

26. Ibid., p. 68.

27. Ibid., pp. 73-74.

28. Randolph E. Paul
Taxation in the United States (Boston: Little, Brown and Company, 1954), p. 10.

29. Ratner, op.cit., p. 85.

30. Ibid., pp. 97-98.

31. Ibid., p. 121.

32. Ibid., pp. 112-13.

33. Ibid. pp. 124-25.

34. Ibid., p. 127.

35. Paul, op.cit., p. 27.

36. Ratner, op.cit., p. 123.

37. Ibid., p. 143.

38. Jeffrey G. Williamson and Peter H. Lindert
American Inequality: A Macroeconomic History (New York: Academic Press, 1980), p. 33.

39. Ratner, op.cit., p. 220.

40. Ibid., p. 221.

41. Joseph J. Thorndike, Jr.
The Very Rich: A History of Wealth (New York: American Heritage/Bananya Books, 1976), p. 53.

42. Paul, op.cit., p. 30.

43. Ibid., p. 30.

44. Ratner, op.cit., p. 151.

45. Ibid., p. 153.

46. Daniel Aaron
Men of Good Hope: A Story of American Progressives (New York: Oxford University Press, 1951), p. 88.

47. Ratner, op.cit., p. 162.

48. Jerold L. Waltman
Political Origins of the U.S. Income Tax (Jackson: University Press of Mississippi, 1985), p. 4.

49. Ratner, op.cit., p. 186.

50. Witte, op.cit., p. 71.

51. Paul, op.cit., p. 35.

52. Ibid., p. 37.

53. Ibid., p. 40.

54. Ratner, op.cit., p. 213.

55. Paul, op.cit., p. 59.

56. Ratner, op.cit., p. 217.

57. Ibid., p. 237.

58. Paul, op.cit., p. 66.

59. Ibid., pp. 88-9.

60. Ratner, p. 298.

61. Ibid., p. 304.

62. Witte, op.cit., pp. 76-78.

63. Paul, op.cit., p. 103.

64. Ibid., p. 108.

65. Alan A. Tait *The Taxation of Personal Wealth* (Urbana: University of Illinois Press, 1967), p. 11.

66. Ratner, op.cit., p. 355.

67. Ibid., p. 356.

68. Waltman, op.cit., p. 78.

69. Paul, op.cit., pp. 107-08.

70. *Congressional Record*, May 16, 1917, p. 2403.

71. Ibid.

72. Ibid.

73. Waltman, op.cit., p. 45.

74. *Congressional Record*, May 16, 1917, p. 2404.

75. Ibid.

76. Witte, op.cit., p. 84.

77. Paul, op.cit., p. 120.

78. Ratner, op.cit., p. 364.

79. Witte, op.cit., p. 85.

80. Ibid., p. 86.

81. Paul, op.cit., p. 165.

82. Ibid., p. 153.

83. Witte, op.cit., p. 97.

84. Ronald A. Mulder, *The Insurgent Progressives in the United States Senate and the New Deal, 1933-1939* (New York: Garland Publishing, Inc., 1979), p. 67.

85. Ibid.

86. *Congressional Record*, May 9, 1933, p. 1100.

87. Ibid.

88. Howard Zinn, editor, *New Deal Thought* (Indianapolis: Bobbs-Merrill, 1966), p. 394.

89. Mulder, op.cit., pp. 116-17.

90. Paul, op.cit., pp. 183-84.

91. Ibid., p. 184.

92. Witte, op.cit., p. 101.

93. Mulder, op.cit., p. 122.

94. Davis, op.cit., p. 253.

95. Bennett, op.cit., p. 128.

96. Ratner, op.cit., pp. 512-13.

97. Ibid., p. 495.

98. Ibid., p. 508.

99. Ibid., p. 562.

100. Paul, op.cit., p. 301.

101. Ibid., p. 302.

102. Ibid., p. 301.

103. Ibid., p. 306.

104. Ibid., p. 313.

105. Witte, op.cit., pp. 116-18.

106. Ibid., p. 117.

107. Paul, op.cit., p. 319.

108. Witte, op.cit., p. 175.

109. Paul, op.cit., p. 318.

110. Witte, op.cit., p. 125.

111. Ibid., p. 128.

112. Paul, op.cit., p. 395.

113. Ibid., pp. 415-421.

114. Witte, op.cit., p. 132.

115. Paul, op.cit., p. 461.

116. Paul, op.cit., p. 466.

117. Ibid., pp. 471-72.

118. Ibid., p. 480.

119. Ibid., p. 494.

120. Ibid., p. 501.

121. Ibid., p. 567.

122. Ibid., p. 616.

123. Witte, op.cit., p. 159.

124. Robert Theobold, editor *The Guaranteed Income: Next Step in Economic Evolution?* (Garden City: Doubleday & Company, Inc., 1966), p. 229.

125. Leslie Lenkowsky *Politics, Economics, and Welfare Reform: The Failure of the Negative Income Tax in Britain and the United States* (Lanham: University Press of America, 1986), p. 2.

126. Herbert Gans "More Equality: Income and Taxes" in Helen Icken Safa and Gloria Levitas, eds., *Social Problems in Corporate America* (New York: Harper & Row, 1975), p. 335.

127. Ibid., p. 341.

128. The decade of negative income tax debate did leave one legacy, the Earned Income Tax Credit enacted in 1975 to help poor families with children. The credit originally "equalled 10 percent of the first $4,000 of earned income." Poor taxpayers with children could claim a 1991 credit of up to 17.3 percent on their first $7,140 of income. The credit is refundable. If the amount of credit exceeds a poor family's actual income tax liability, the family is entitled to a check for the difference. See the *1991 Green Book*, Committee on Ways and Means (Washington, D.C.: U.S. House of Representatives, 1991), pp. 897-890.

129. Witte, op.cit., p. 217.

130. Ibid., p. 221.

131. Quoted in Witte, ibid., p. 22.

132. Ibid., p. 222.

133. In 1989, the 86 nations with an income tax levied an average top rate of 47 percent. See John Miller and James Goodno, "Much Ado About Nothing," *Dollars & Sense*, December 1990, p. 16.

134. Ibid., p. 20.

135. Ibid., p. 375.

136. Joseph A. Pechman and Benjamin A. Okner *Who Bears the Tax Burden?* (Washington, D.C.: The Brookings Institution, 1974), p. 10.

137. Witte, op.cit., pp. 369-70.

138. William M. Dugger "The Wealth Tax: A Policy Proposal," *Journal of Economic Issues*, March 1990, p.141.

139. Ravi Batra "Wealth Tax on Top 1 Percent of the Population," *Prout Journal*, Summer 1989, pp. 10-11.

140. Mortimer Lipsky *A Tax on Wealth* (Cranberry, N.J.: A.S. Barnes and Company, 1977), p. 164.

141. Ibid., p. 159.

142. Ibid., pp. 172-73.

143. Ibid., p. 177.

3. The TenTimesRule

How rich is too rich? As a society, we seldom ask.

We ask the converse question—how poor is too poor?—all the time. As a matter of fact, our nation has officially determined exactly how poor is too poor. We have set a poverty line. If you don't reach that line, you're too poor and, as such, entitled to special services.

We've also established a minimum wage. Anyone who labors, we as a nation believe, deserves a basic level of compensation.

The poverty line and the minimum wage reflect America's commitment to eradicate poverty. In theory at least, we seek a society without poor people, a society where every one can live at least in minimal decency.

In practice, we pay this commitment no more than lip service. The minimum wage constantly lags badly behind inflation. Programs for the very poor are squeezed and slashed as a matter of course. Yet the basic consensus remains. Only a few cranks question our basic commitment, as a society, to end the indecency of abject poverty.

No such commitment exists at the other end of the economic spectrum. The indecency of profligate wealth goes largely unchallenged. Despite a century of trying, we Americans have yet to ade-

quately limit wealth. The income tax, once the pride and joy of patriots who feared plutocracy, has become just another oppressive levy on working people. Inheritance and estate taxes barely make a dent on the vast wealth handed down from one wealthy generation to the next. Proposals for taxing wealth itself—the value of stock holdings, for instance—generate little enthusiasm, not surprisingly since the only tax on wealth most Americans have ever experienced is the widely detested property tax.

Meanwhile, amid all these failures to limit the accumulation of great fortunes, the gap between rich people and everybody else grows ever wider. Between 1980 and 1990, America's wealthiest 1 percent of families boosted their share of the nation's income by over 30 percent.[1]

What can we do to get back on track? Maybe we need to go back to fundamentals. Maybe we need to revisit our most basic assumptions.

We as a society, for instance, assume that decency demands an official poverty line. But why just a *poverty* line? Why not a *wealth* line, too? We have a floor on income, the minimum wage. Why not a ceiling? If a minimum wage can help solve the poor people problem, why not establish a *maximum* wage to help solve the rich people problem?

A maximum wage. An impossible pipedream? The minimum wage must have once seemed equally fantastic. Yet today we take the concept of a minimum wage for granted. The republic is better for it. Why not a maximum wage?

Down through the years, a variety of Americans have directly posed this question. Thomas Paine, the great pamphleteer of the American Revolution, called for a "tax on estates" that would limit any individual's income to no more than £12,369.[2] In World

War I, as we have seen, reformers who counted in their ranks members of Congress wanted annual incomes capped at no more than $100,000. A generation later, after the start of World War II, Franklin Roosevelt asked Congress to tax away all income over $25,000.

None of these proposals for a maximum wage went very far. FDR's New Deal could push a minimum wage through Congress. It couldn't even get a maximum wage proposal out of committee. But, in another sense, both the maximum wage *and* the minimum wage have failed. The maximum wage has never made it into law. The minimum wage, which has been enacted into law, no longer guarantees what its original advocates so clearly wanted: a minimum level of decency for all people who labor. In fact, at the current $4.25 hourly minimum, a minimum wage worker who supports two dependents would fall $2,000 short of the official federal poverty line.

Is the maximum wage an impossible pipedream? The minimum wage must have once seemed equally fantastic. Yet today we take the concept of a minimum wage for granted.

Political analysts sometimes contrast the erosion of the minimum wage—and the woeful underfunding of other programs meant to help America's poorest people—with the outstanding success of Social Security. Social Security benefits have actually kept pace with inflation. Few politicians today would even think of suggesting a Social Security cutback. What makes Social Security so unassailable and anti-poverty programs such tempting targets? One simple reality: Social Security benefits a broad cross-spectrum of Americans, low- as well as middle-income. But the benefits of anti-poverty programs, such as they are, go only to those officially defined as poor. Indeed, in some cases, Americans just above the poverty threshold are actually penalized for their relative good fortune. A mother below a specifically defined low-income line can count on Medicaid for her sick child.

A mother over that line is on her own. Is it any wonder that working Americans above the poverty line, Americans who struggle to get by, so often resent those below the line? Is it any wonder that the political base for maintaining decency for poor people is so narrow?

Any attempt to place a ceiling on the income of the wealthy would have to face the same political challenge that confronts attempts to place an adequate income floor under the poor. To become politically viable, a maximum wage proposal couldn't just cap the income of the wealthy. To become politically viable, a maximum wage proposal would have to offer direct benefits to the non-wealthy, just as Social Security offers direct benefits to the non-poor.

In years past, maximum wage advocates have never adequately explained how a maximum wage might benefit the non-wealthy. In fact, in 1942, when Franklin Roosevelt proposed his maximum wage ceiling on the incomes of the rich, he also proposed, at the same time, a tax hike on the non-rich majority.

What if Roosevelt had tried the reverse? What if he had coupled a proposal to raise taxes on the wealthy with a proposal to lower taxes on everyone else? What if Roosevelt had argued that only by imposing a maximum wage on the very wealthy could the nation afford a better life for ordinary Americans?

Might this approach have created a different political dynamic? We can actually answer this question with a fair degree of confidence. Just a half-dozen years before FDR's maximum wage proposal, Huey Long did exactly what Roosevelt did not. Long proposed a cap on the income of the wealthy and then directly linked his proposed cap to the improved well-being of the non-wealthy majority. If his plan became law, Huey Long promised, every family would be guaranteed $5,000 and every qualified child a college education. The very slogan Long adopted for his tax-the-rich campaign—"every man a king"—emphasized the benefits that capping wealth and income would bring the vast majority of Americans.

Long's approach to the maximum wage, unlike Roosevelt's, did capture the public imagination. The lesson for today should be obvious. Any plan to raise taxes significantly on the income of the wealthy, to become politically viable, must clearly and directly benefit the non-wealthy. Any maximum wage proposal that seeks to make a serious political impact must link the well-being of the vast majority of Americans to the imposition of the maximum wage.

And what could that link be? What could be simpler—and make more common sense—than linking a proposed maximum wage to the already existing minimum wage?

The maximum wage, if we take this approach, would be some multiple of the minimum. Any amount of income earned above this multiple would be taxed away.

But what about the vast majority of Americans above the minimum and below the maximum? How would a maximum wage tied to the minimum wage be in their interest?

The maximum wage would benefit this vast group of Americans if the same new tax law that taxed away any income above the maximum wage *reduced* taxes for everyone below it.

For the moment, let's be arbitrary. Let's set our maximum wage at ten times the minimum. Our maximum wage proposal could then be expressed as a very simple proposition:

> No person in the United States shall be permitted to earn more than ten times the income earned by any other person.

Any plan to raise taxes significantly on the income of the wealthy, to become politically viable, must clearly and directly benefit the non-wealthy.

What would this Ten Times Rule mean for American taxpayers? Let's use 1990 as our reference year. In 1990, the minimum wage stood at $3.80 per hour. For the sake of round numbers, let's calculate that minimum at $4. At this hourly rate, over a year of 50 working weeks, a minimum-wage employee would earn $8,000.

Ten times this $8,000 minimum would amount to $80,000. If the Ten Times Rule were suddenly to become the law of the land, then no single individual would be allowed to keep any annual income over $80,000. Any income above that $80,000 "maximum wage" would be subject to a 100 percent annual tax.

For a couple filing jointly, the maximum wage would be $160,000, ten times the income of a couple working at the minimum wage. Any income above $160,000 on a joint return would be totally taxed away.

And income below the ten times limit? Under the Ten Times Rule, taxes on this income would also be tied to the minimum wage, on a rate scale from one to ten. A person earning the minimum wage would pay a 1 percent income tax. A person earning five times the minimum wage would pay income tax at a 5 percent rate. A person earning ten times the minimum wage would pay a 10 percent tax. The result: true tax simplification—and significant tax cuts for everyone below the maximum wage limits.

Questions immediately abound. Why "ten times"? Why not a maximum wage at five times the minimum—or five hundred? How many Americans would actually see lower taxes under the Ten Times Rule? How many would see their taxes go higher? Would the Ten Times Rule be "fiscally responsible"? Would raising taxes on the rich—and lowering them for everyone else—bring in enough revenue to keep the government running?

Let's take these questions one at a time.

Why a *Ten* Times Rule?

How much inequality of wealth and income should a decent society tolerate?

In 1688, England's 300 temporal lords averaged 300 times their countrymen's median income.[3]

Three hundred years later, in 1988, American junk bond kingpin Michael Milken made $500 million. In the same year, America's Teacher of the Year earned $36,000, fourteen thousand times less than Milken.[4]

Halfway across the world, Mikhail Gorbachev took home 1,500 rubles a month in 1988, seven times the average Soviet worker's salary.[5]

Seven times? Three hundred times? Fourteen thousand times? Just what is the proper ratio for decency?

At the turn of the century, George Bernard Shaw argued eloquently that decency demands total income equality. Shaw contended that "no stable civilization is possible without the rigid maintenance of equality of income for every individual."[6] His critics argued in response that total equality would eliminate all economic incentive and destroy any hope for the progress so necessary to improve civilized life.

But how much inequality is necessary to generate incentives? Economists have debated this question for quite some time, without reaching anything close to a consensus. This failure to reach consensus, noted economist W. S. Vickrey a generation ago, shouldn't surprise anyone. "At one extreme, complete equality may be held to produce a low aggregate output, whether from lack

Under the Ten Times Rule, a person earning ten times the minimum wage would pay a 10 percent income tax. Any income over the maximum would be taxed at a 100 percent rate.

of incentives or for other reasons," he explained. "At the other extreme, there is presumably some degree of inequality that would give the maximum total product."

Few egalitarians, Vickrey added, "would be so extreme as to insist on total equality regardless of the degree to which this would reduce the total product to be shared, and perhaps few rugged individualists would insist on the maximum total product (assuming this can be defined!), regardless of how unequal the corresponding distribution."

The entire question, Vickrey concluded, "is an ethical problem on which individuals have differed widely." Economists, he noted, are little help here: "The economist hardly knows even how to go about finding an answer, or how to start to appraise the merits of alternative answers."[7]

The philosophers, for their part, have never shirked this debate. Plato in *The Laws*, for instance, pronounced the ideal ratio between the wealth of the richest and the wealth of the poorest to be four to one. For Aristotle, the appropriate ratio was five to one.[8]

The philosophical dialogue on inequality of wealth and income continues unabated. "Today, certainly," noted John Arthur and William Shaw in 1978, "the problem of what constitutes a just economic distribution is central to social and political philosophy."[9]

"Entitlement" theorists solve this problem simply. They argue that "a person deserves goods because of some action the person has taken or some trait the person possesses."[10] Period. If you earn it, you deserve it. That's economic justice.

"Welfarist" philosophers consider this approach far too narrow. For these theorists, what counts is the overall well-being, or

welfare, of a society. For those welfarists known as utilitarians, for instance, there is "only one moral issue: which course of action promotes the greatest sum of happiness for all concerned?" The most just distribution of economic goods is the distribution that "produces more happiness than any other."[11]

All sorts of nuances divide philosophers in the welfarist camp. For some, social welfare is simply the sum of individual happiness in a society. These philosophers don't particularly care how wealth is distributed within this sum.[12] Other philosophers "would accept a reduction in the total amount of welfare in a society in exchange of improving the welfare of society's less well off members."[13] Still others argue that "group welfare is at an optimum when it is impossible to make any one person better off without at the same time making at least one other person worse off."[14]

John Rawls, a contemporary American philosopher, confronts inequality from a somewhat different perspective. His "difference principle" maintains that inequalities, or differences in income and wealth, are "justified only if the inequalities increase the well-being of the least advantaged members of the society."[15]

"Minimum sacrifice" theorists, for their part, start from the utilitarian principle that "law should be designed to bring about the greatest good to the greatest number."[16] A society that adopted minimum sacrifice as its guiding light would tax the wealthy—and keep on taxing the wealthy—as long as the dollars taken from them "involve less sacrifice" than dollars taken from citizens less wealthy. "The mimimum sacrifice theory would, if it could," notes tax historian Randolph Paul, "proceed to the destination of 100 percent marginal tax rates."[17]

Minimum sacrifice, in short, leads us toward the concept of a

> *Plato pronounced the ideal ratio between the wealth of the richest and the wealth of the poorest to be four to one. For Aristotle, the appropriate ratio was five to one.*

maximum wage. But none of this lofty philosophizing helps us determine just what that maximum, in a decent society, ought to be. For that guidance, we need to descend to the data and examine how societies, in real life, actually distribute income and wealth.

The eminent English scholar, Henry Phelps Brown, understands these realities as well as anyone. He has devoted a lifetime of research to studying how societies allocate wealth and income. In his earlier days, Phelps Brown always had difficulty translating his wealth and income distribution data into clear and useful information for lay people—until he came across the "Pen parade," a playful conceptual device developed by Dutch economist Jan Pen.

Pen asked his readers to visualize income distribution as a parade, with the marchers "endowed with heights proportional to their incomes." Leading off the parade would be a society's lowest-income individuals. The multi-millionaires would pull up the rear.

In a Pen parade, marchers who earned a society's median income would stand at normal height. If the total march lasted an hour, we wouldn't see these normal-height people for a half hour. They would be preceded by a "parade of dwarfs." Meanwhile, at the back of the parade, a few multi-millionaires would peer down at the line of march ahead of them. This would be one long peer. The multi-millionaires would have their heads in the clouds.[18]

This Pen parade can easily be converted into a diagram, going left to right, with a line tracing the heads of our paraders. Phelps Brown has assembled "Pen parade" diagrams for all sorts of different societies, at all sorts of different times. Societies, Phelps Brown has discovered, all parade alike.

Phelps Brown divides his Pen parade diagrams into horizontal percentiles, with the poorest marchers in the first percentile and the richest in the 100th. In his diagrams, each society's line of march moves upward as we move from left to right. What's most significant is just how steeply the line rises.

In all the societies Phelps Brown has paraded, income distribution moves up as a modestly sloping straight line between the lowest and the 85th percentile. Up to the 85th percentile, notes Phelps Brown, any differences in income "between one person and another person present themselves as a steady and gentle gradation." In the range of incomes between the poorest 1 percent and the 85th percentile, there are no big gaps. Each person within this range "rubs elbows with others who are a little better or worse off than he or she is."[19]

Above the 85th percentile, everything changes. The gentle slope starts a precipitous incline, until, at the highest percentile, our gentle hill has become a nearly impossible vertical ascent.

Why do income gradations, so proportionate one to the other below the 85th percentile, become so steep above it? Below the 85th percentile, Phelps Brown explains, incomes largely reflect the actual work people do. Above the 85th percentile, incomes start reflecting not income from jobs, but the return from property rents, interest from bonds, dividends from stocks, speculative gains. The gentle slope between the first and 85th percentile reappears so consistently in one society after another that Phelps Brown considers this "smoothness of gradation not as a statistical artefact but as a social reality."[20] For Phelps Brown, the gentle slope of inequality between the first and 85th percentiles reflects the natural order of economic life, a natural order that reappears in societies as disparate as the United States and the Soviet Union, Sweden and Peru.

At the highest levels, incomes start reflecting not income from jobs, but the return from property rents, bond interest, stock dividends, and speculative gains.

But incomes above the 85th percentile don't follow the same gentle slope, and the slopes of these incomes do vary from society to society. These high incomes reflect profits from property, not wages from work. Incomes that recipients earn by actual work, Phelps Brown notes, can claim to be justified by the contribution the recipients have made. "But what contribution to the community," asks Phelps Brown, "can be set against the fortune that is made by speculation, or is simply inherited?"[21]

A decent society, Phelps Brown's work suggests, would not tolerate the wealth and income disparities created by these fortunes. A decent society would limit itself to the level of inequality that appears between the first and 85th percentiles in every society's Pen parade. And what is the income ratio between the first and 85th percentile in these Pen parades? Give or take a dollar or mark or pound or ruble or two, that ratio is ten to one.

Observe for yourself. The ten-to-one ratio, once you begin looking for it, emerges everywhere in the world of real work. Noted Yale law professor Boris Bittker in 1978: "In virtually all institutions of our society—the universities with which we are especially familiar, the federal civil service, and business organizations save at the very top—the salary scale from bottom to top is confined to a ratio of 1 to 10 or thereabouts."[22]

Why not make this ten-to-one ratio the foundation for our maximum wage? If the Ten Times Rule were to become the law of the land, then those who actually work would be rewarded within the income continuum that reappears again and again in all modern societies. What would not be rewarded in a Ten Times land would be speculation or any other activity that brings income without effort.

We ought not leave this discussion without noting one fascinating coincidence from centuries past. In 1427, the Florentine republic enacted a tax that has gone down in history as "a vast advance in social justice." This Florentine tax "fell substantially on the well-to-do."[23] That tax was known as *la decima scalata*.[24] In English, historians call this tax simply "the Tenth."

American Incomes and the Ten Times Rule

If the Ten Times Rule were the law of the land, if all income above the maximum wage were taxed away, then clearly those Americans above the maximum wage would pay more taxes, much more. But how many Americans would have their incomes cut down in size by the Ten Times Rule maximum? And how about the Americans whose incomes fall under the Ten Times Rule maximum? What would the Ten Times Rule mean to the incomes of these Americans?

Tables 2 and 3 attempt to answer these questions. Table 2 divides American taxpaying families into income tenths, or deciles, as the statisticians like to say. The table indicates, for each decile, the average 1990 pretax income, then the federal income tax paid on that income in 1990, both as a percent and as a dollar total.

Table 3 notes what the same taxpayers would have paid in 1990 if the Ten Times Rule had been the rule of the land, then compares how each income level of taxpayers fares under existing law in 1990 and under the Ten Times Rule.

Both tables subdivide the richest tenth of American families into the richest 1 percent, the next richest 4 percent, and the next richest 5 percent.

What do our tables tell us? Under the Ten Times Rule, the

What would not be rewarded in a Ten Times land would be speculation or any other acitivity that brings income without effort.

**THE TEN TIMES RULE: WHAT DIFFERENCE WOULD IT
MAKE ON YOUR TAX BILL?**

Table 2
FEDERAL INCOME TAXES DUE UNDER 1990 TAX RATES

Income Level By Decilie	Avg 1990 Income	1990 Rate	Avg 1990 Tax Paid
Lowest	$ 4,695	-2.5%*	NA
Second	10,154	-1.1	NA
Third	16,363	2.2	359.99
Fourth	22,492	4.5	1,012.14
Fifth	28,123	6.1	1,715.50
Sixth	33,760	7.2	2,430.72
Seventh	40,651	8.3	3,374.03
Eighth	49,049	9.6	4,708.70
Ninth	63,663	11.6	7,384.33
Next 5%	82,154	13.2	10,844.33
Next 4%	125,800	16.3	20,505.40
Next 1%	548,969	21.5	118,028.34

*The negative rates reflect the federal Earned Income Tax Credit, which applies to poor families with children.

Source: Congressional Budget Office Tax Simulation Model, *1990 Green Book*, Committee on Ways and Means, pp. 1186-1189.

Table 3
1990 INCOME TAXES UNDER THE TEN TIMES RULE

Income By Decile	10X Rule Tax Rate*	10X Rule Tax Paid	1990 Tax Savings (Loss) If 10X Rule in Effect
Lowest	0	0.00	0.00
Second	0	0.00	0.00
Third	1	163.63	196.36
Fourth	1	224.92	787.22
Fifth	1	281.23	1,434.27
Sixth	2	675.20	1,755.52
Seventh	2	813.02	2,561.01
Eighth	3	1,471.47	3,237.23
Ninth	3	1,909.89	5,475.02
Next 5%	5	4,107.70	6,736.63
Next 4%	7	8,806.00	11,699.40
Next 1%	74	404,969.00	(286,940.66)

* The Ten Times Rule tax rate would be keyed to the minimum wage. This table assumes an $8,000 annual income for a minimum wage worker. A husband and wife with a joint income of $33,760—the average for the sixth income decile—would pay a Ten Times Rule tax rate of 2 percent since the family's $33,760 income would be two times the annual income of a family with two minimum wage earners.

richest 1 percent of American families would pay more in taxes, a great deal more. Every other taxpaying family would pay less. Most would see their federal income tax bill drop by far more than half.

The poorest American families pay no federal income taxes under current law. That wouldn't change under the Ten Times Rule. The changes would begin with those families struggling at just above the poverty line.

In 1990, American families averaging $16,363 paid 2.2 percent, about $360, of that total in federal income tax. Under the Ten Times Rule, these same families would have paid only 1 percent of their income in taxes—because, in Ten Times Rule America, $16,000 would be the minimum annual wage for a couple filing jointly. Total tax savings for a family earning $16,363: $196.36.

Move up the income scale and the tax savings become even more striking. A family that earned $28,123 in 1990—the average income in the fifth decile—paid $1,715 in federal income tax. If the Ten Times Rule had been in effect in 1990, this same family would have paid $281 in federal income tax, an 83 percent tax savings.

More comfortable families would see similar savings. American families in the ninth decile averaged $63,663 in 1990, about what a household headed by two veteran public school teachers would have earned. In 1990, a family earning $63,663 paid $7,384 in federal income tax.

Under the Ten Times Rule, this family's federal income tax bill would have been less than $2,000!

What about America's richest 10 percent? The Ten Times Rule would actually lower taxes for nine out of ten families at this lof-

If the Ten Times Rule were law, most taxpaying families would see their federal income tax bill drop by far more than half.

tiest of levels.

Families that averaged $125,800 in 1990 made more money than 95 percent of America's families. A typical family that brought home $125,800 in 1990 paid $20,505 of that total in federal income tax. But under the Ten Times Rule this same family would have paid $11,699 less.

Now we're at the summit, the richest 1 percent of American families. A vast chasm separates these Americans from the rest of us. In 1990, this top 1 percent averaged an incredible $549,000, *more than four times as much as the next highest 4 percent of*

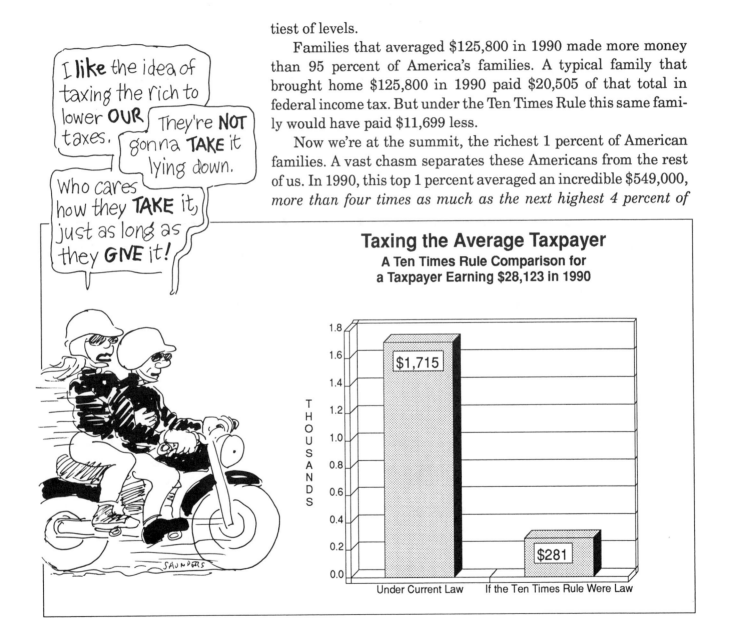

I **like** the idea of taxing the rich to lower **OUR** taxes.

They're **NOT** gonna **TAKE** it lying down.

Who cares how they **TAKE** it, just as long as they **GIVE** it!

Taxing the Average Taxpayer
A Ten Times Rule Comparison for a Taxpayer Earning $28,123 in 1990

THOUSANDS

Under Current Law	If the Ten Times Rule Were Law
$1,715	$281

families.

In 1990, this top 1 percent, the truly wealthy, paid federal income taxes at a 21.5 percent rate. The total 1990 federal income tax bill for the average family in the top 1 percent: $118,028.

Under the Ten Times Rule, the tax calculations for these richest Americans would have been quite a bit different. On the first $160,000 of these families' income—ten times the minimum annual joint income under the Ten Times Rule—the federal tax would have been 10 percent. On our super-wealthy families' remaining annual income of $388,969, the tax rate would have

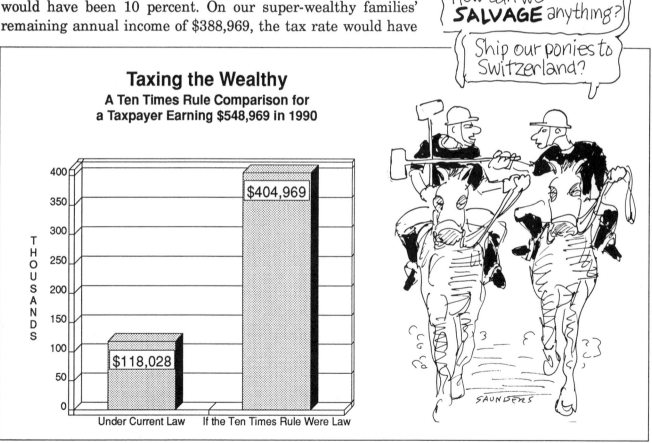

Taxing the Wealthy

A Ten Times Rule Comparison for a Taxpayer Earning $548,969 in 1990

THOUSANDS

$404,969

$118,028

Under Current Law   If the Ten Times Rule Were Law

been 100 percent. Total tax bill: over $404,000, an increase of $286,000 over what the average American family in the top 1 percent paid in 1990 under existing law.

Step back from these figures and what do you see? In 1990, had the Ten Times Rule been the law of the land:

- the bottom 20 percent of American taxpaying families would have paid no federal income tax at all.

- the next 30 percent would have paid 1 percent of their income in federal income tax.

- the next 39 percent would have paid from $1,750 to $12,000 less in taxes.

- the richest Americans would have seen their tax bills rise by over 300 percent!

Can America Afford the Ten Times Rule?

Tax breaks for 99 percent of Americans, a tax increase on only the very, very rich. The Ten Times Rule is one tax formula with political appeal. But would the Ten Times Rule be fiscally "responsible"? Would the increased taxes on the wealthy under the Ten Times Rule raise enough revenue to underwrite a tax cut for everyone else? Or would the Ten Times Rule, if implemented, bankrupt the federal government and leave essential government programs starving for funds—even more so than they are now?

Down through the years, critics have repeatedly argued that leveling the wealth of the rich—to increase the well-being of everyone else—simply doesn't work. There are just too many people in the "everyone else," these critics note, and too few dollars in the hands of the rich.

Contemporary observers, for instance, found Huey Long's Share-Our-Wealth prescription—a ceiling on income and wealth that would raise enough money to ensure every family $5,000— "either demagogic hypocrisy or else economic ignorance so abysmal as to inspire awe."[25] Long, one historian has noted, "would have had to confiscate all incomes over $4,000 to assure a paltry $1,400 to the needy."[26]

A generation after Long, statistician Herman Miller made similar calculations for post-War America. In 1959, Miller computed, 58 million American families and individuals shared one third of a trillion dollars in cash income. If each taxpayer received an equal share of that income, Miller noted, that share "would only be $5,700."[27]

Critics of plans that would cap wealth and income are hardly limited to the ranks of apologists for wealth. Observers left as well as right have blasted what they see as the simplistic and naive assumptions of those who would soak the rich in order to sweeten everyone else's pocket.

"Neither Huey Long nor anybody else can divide up wealth generally in this country or in any country that has passed beyond a purely simple primitive agrarianism," noted Carleton Beals, a prominent progressive journalist in the 1930s. "We need more wealth, not its dissipation or even its redistribution."[28]

Forty years later, Norman B. Ture, soon to become a top Treasury Department official under Ronald Reagan, blasted redistributional thinking from the perspective of the political right.

"While equality of economic status may be a desideratum and

> *Tax breaks for 99 percent of Americans, a tax increase on only the very, very rich. The Ten Times Rule would be one tax formula with political appeal.*

feasible for an impoverished society, its attainment in such a society is of little consequence," Ture noted, "but in our affluent society, where equalizing economic status would be significant, it is neither desirable nor feasible."[29] Is any serious redistribution of wealth in a modern, affluent society simply, as these critics charge, a waste of time? Can limiting the income of the rich significantly help boost the incomes of everyone else, or is any plan that smacks of the maximum wage approach just a cruel hoax that would leave non-rich Americans little better off than they were before redistribution?

Years ago, critics may have had a point when they ridiculed the economics of redistribution. But today, in modern America, the only "cruel hoax" in the redistribution debate is the argument that "soaking the rich" wouldn't do everyone else much good. In the United States today, we *can* afford the Ten Times Rule. In fact, substituting Ten Times Rule tax rates for the current federal income tax rate schedule would actually *increase* federal revenues.

Tables 4 and 5 calculate what federal income revenues would have been in 1990 had the Ten Times Rule been in effect. Table 4 indicates the federal income tax couples filing jointly would have paid in 1990, by income level, and Table 5 offers the same data for single taxpayers.

These tables tell a fascinating story. If Ten Times Rule tax rates had been in effect in 1990, the U.S. Treasury would have collected nearly $463 billion in income taxes from America's wealthiest taxpayers.

This $463 billion nearly *equals* the $467 billion in individual income taxes the IRS collected from all taxpayers in the 1990 federal fiscal year.[30]

Think about that a moment. If the Ten Times Rule had been

law in 1990, nearly all the federal income taxes paid by the bottom 99 percent of taxpayers would have represented an *increase* for the federal government over revenues collected under current law, over $175 billion of increase.

That $175 billion could have erased most of the 1990 federal budget deficit—or, more significantly, gone into programs that would have helped balance America's *social* deficit, the ever-quickening erosion of our schools, our roads, our rails, our air, and our water.

Can we afford, as a fiscally responsible nation, to enact the Ten Times Rule? The question might better be reversed. Can we afford not to?

> *Can limiting the income of the rich significantly help boost the incomes of everyone else? Today, in modern America, the answer is yes.*

Opposing the Ten Times Rule

If a campaign to enact a Ten Times Rule ever did become politically significant, the campaign *against* the Ten Times Rule would quickly trot out a wide variety of counter arguments.

Some arguments against more egalitarian distributions of income have been around so long they've become pseudo-folk wisdom. The maximum wage, we would be told, would inhibit individuals from going as far as their energies will take them. The task of eliminating great economic inequalities would create a "horrible bureaucratic structure." Leveling incomes would create a bland, uniform society devoid of excitement.[31]

More scholarly critics would charge that the maximum wage would make our society less productive. "Very large output losses," charged William J. Baumol in a 1986 book, *Superfairness*, "are likely to accompany any attempt to get anywhere *very close* to equality."[32]

THE TEN TIMES RULE: WHAT WOULD HAPPEN TO FEDERAL REVENUES?

Table 4
FEDERAL INCOME TAX REVENUE, 1990, FROM COUPLES FILING JOINTLY, HAD TEN TIMES RULE TAX RATES BEEN IN EFFECT

Income Level	Pretax Income	Number Joint (000s)	10X Tax On Joint	Joint Tax Total
Lowest 10%	$ 4,695	1,003	$0.00	$0
Second 10%	10,154	3,456	0.00	0
Third 10%	16,363	4,125	163.63	674,973,750
Fourth 10%	22,492	5,797	224.92	1,303,861,240
Fifth 10%	28,123	5,797	281.23	1,630,290,310
Sixth 10%	33,760	8,473	675.20	5,720,969,600
Seventh 10%	40,651	8,473	813.02	6,888,718,460
Eighth 10%	49,049	8,473	1,471.47	12,467,765,310
Nine 10%	63,663	9,922	1,909.89	18,949,928,580
Next 5%	82,154	4,961	4,107.70	20,378,299,700
Next 4%	125,800	3,835	8,806.00	33,771,010,000
Next 1%	548,969	958	404,969.00	387,960,302,000

Total $489,746,118,950

Table 5
FEDERAL INCOME TAX REVENUE, 1990, FROM SINGLE FILERS, UNDER THE TEN TIMES RULE, WITH OVERALL TOTALS FOR ALL TAXPAYERS

Pretax Income Level	Single Returns (000s)	10X Tax	Total On Single	Overall 10X Tax Revenues Joint & Single
$ 4,695	10,146	$0	$0	$0
10,154	7,693	102	81,116,758	781,116,758
16,363	7,024	327	2,298,576,062	2,973,549,812
22,492	5,352	450	2,407,408,728	3,711,269,968
28,123	5,252	844	4,515,175,773	6,145,466,083
33,760	2,676	1,350	3,613,265,280	9,334,234,880
40,651	2,676	2,032	5,438,494,035	12,327,212,495
49,049	2,676	2,943	7,874,424,558	20,342,189,868
63,663	1,227	4,456	5,466,678,147	24,416,606,727
82,154	613	10,154	6,227,955,900	26,606,255,600
125,800	624	53,800	33,597,024,000	67,368,034,000
548,969	157	476,969	74,822,127,030	462,782,429,030

Total Ten Times Rule Revenue Collected   **$636,788,365,221**

Sources: These figures apply the total number of 1990 taxpayers (*Statistics of Income Bulletin*, Winter 1989-90, p. 97) against existing joint-single taxpayer ratios (*Statistics of Income Bulletin*, Summer, 1988, p. 11). Pretax income breakdowns are from the Congressional Budget Office Tax Simulation Model (*1990 Green Book*, Committee on Ways and Means, pp. 1186-1189.) See note 33.

Many democratically inclined critics, for their part, would see the Ten Times Rule as a hopeless deadend, as long as the basic structure of America's economy goes unchallenged.

"The striking differences in income and wealth which serve as a roadblock to egalitarian democracy cannot be obliterated merely by the passage of legislation," noted Richard Parker in a 1972 book that decried inequality in America. "Workers must be paid in unequal scales in order to make them do unpleasant work, just as the owners of capital must be given huge rewards in order to make them invest. No amount of legislation in a private economy can change this economic fact of life."[34]

All these critics might even be right. The Ten Times Rule, if it ever became the law of the land, might make America less interesting and less productive. The Ten Times Rule might insert too much government into economic life. The Ten Times Rule might outrageously frustrate America's most talented and creative people.

But these are not the only possibilities. The Ten Times Rule, if enacted, might start a chain reaction that would build America up, not break America down, a chain reaction that might create a new America.

We need now to peer into the future and explore *these* possibilities.

Notes

1. Lawrence Mishel and David M. Frankel *The State of Working America, 1990-91 Edition* (Washington, D.C.: Economic Policy Institute, 1990), p. 271.

2. Henry Phelps Brown *Egalitarianism and the Generation of Inequality* (Oxford: Clarendon Press, 1988), p. 139.

3. Ibid., p. 310.

4. Molly Ivins "Deep Voodoo," *Mother Jones*, January/February 1991, p. 10.

5. "Soviet Editor Reveals Gorbachev's Pay & Perks," *The Washington Post*, February 1, 1989, pp. D1, D11.

6. George Bernard Shaw *The Road to Equality: Ten Unpublished Lectures and Essays, 1884-1918* (Boston: Beacon Press, 1971), p. 166.

7. W. S. Vickrey "An Exchange of Questions between Economics and Philosophy" in Edmund S. Phelps, ed., *Economic Justice: Selected Readings* (Baltimore: Penguin Education, 1973), pp. 38-39.

8. Brown, op.cit., p. 19.

9. John Arthur and William H. Shaw, editors *Justice and Economic Distribution* (Englewood Cliffs, N.J.: Prentice-Hall, Inc., 1978), p ix.

10. Joseph Bankman and Thomas Griffith "Social Welfare and the Rate Structure," *California Law Review*, December 1987, p. 1916.

11. Arthur and Shaw, op.cit., p 7.

12. Bankman and Griffith, op.cit., p. 1949.

13. Ibid.

14. John Rawls "Distributive Justice," in Edmund S. Phelps, ed., *Economic Justice: Selected Readings* (Baltimore: Penguin Education, 1973), p. 325. Not the Rawls' view.

15. Bankman and Griffith, op.cit., p. 1949fn.

16. Randolph E. Paul *Taxation in the United States* (Boston: Little, Brown and Company, 1954), p. 733.

17. Ibid., p. 734.

18. Brown, op.cit., page 268.

19. Ibid., p. 465.

20. Ibid., p. 466.

21. Ibid., p. 308.

22. Boris I. Bittker comments on the Principal Paper by Norman B. Ture in Arleen A. Leibowitz, ed., *Wealth Redistribution and the Income Tax* (Lexington: Lexington Books, 1977), p. 67.

23. Ferdinand Schevill *History of Florence from the Founding of the City through the Renaissance* (New York: Frederick Ungar Publishing Co., 1961), p. 346.

24. Paul, op.cit., p. 721.

25. Carleton Beals *The Story of Huey P. Long* (Westport: Greenwood Press, 1935, 1971), p. 312.

26. David H. Bennett *Demagogues in the Depression* (New Brunswick, New Jersey: Rutgers University Press, 1969), p. 121.

27. Herman P. Miller *Rich Man, Poor Man* (New York: Thomas Y. Crowell Company, 1964), p. 1.

28. Carleton Beals, op. cit., p. 312.

29. Norman B. Ture Principal Paper, in Leibowitz, op.cit., p. 5.

30. *The Economic and Budget Outlook: Fiscal Years 1992-1996.* Congressional Budget Office. Washington, D.C. January, 1991.

31. Jennifer L. Hochschild *What's Fair?: American Beliefs about Distributive Justice* (Cambridge: Harvard University Press, 1981), p. 41

32. William J. Baumol *Superfairness: Applications and Theory* (Cambridge: MIT Press, 1986), p. 193.

33. Other estimates suggest lower maximum wage revenues from the rich. In 1989, the congressional Joint Committee on Taxation concluded that a 100 percent tax on incomes over $200,000 would raise $204 billion in 1990. Maximum wage revenue estimates will vary by how "taxable income" is defined. Tables 4 and 5 use the CBO income statistics, which do not subtract from pretax income paper losses incurred for tax purposes. These tables also assume a Ten Times rate structure without tax exemptions, deductions, or credits. Chapter 4 discusses allowing tax breaks for charitable contributions and state and local government bond interest. See *1990 Green Book*, pp. 1164-5.

34. See Richard Parker *The Myth of the Middle Class* (New York: Liveright, 1972), p. 206.

4. Life in Ten Times Rule America

What would life be like in Ten Times Rule America? How different would our lives actually be if no American could earn more than ten times the income earned by any other American?

Very different. We live in a society, after all, where the presence of rich people distorts nearly every aspect of daily life. Remove that presence and the impact would be felt in society's every sphere.

In fact, we might do well to start our examination of Ten Times Rule America by looking at America's favorite sphere: the baseball. What better place to begin than our national pastime.

The Ten Times Rule and the Old Ballgame

In Ten Times Rule America, baseball would be fundamentally different. Not the game, of course. Not the thrill of a bottom-of-the-ninth rally. Not the grace of a double play. What would change would be everything else. The Ten Times Rule would eliminate the distractions and the aggravations that inevitably accompany baseball as a business practiced by rich people.

If the Ten Times Rule were to become the law of the land, the most obvious baseball casualty would be the multi-million dollar ballplayer salary. Under the Ten Times Rule, any salary over ten times the minimum wage would be taxed away. Today, even utility infielders make more money than ten times the minimum wage—much more.

Under the Ten Times Rule, multi-million dollar annual salaries would go the way of cheap homeruns in the Polo Grounds. Ballclubs would still have to compete in the free agent market for ballplayers, but the terms of the competition would drastically change. Instead of megabuck three-year annual contracts, teams would have to come up with new incentives for wooing ballplayers. Some might guarantee players front-office jobs—and decent incomes—after their playing days are over.

Other teams might compete for ballplayers by making contributions to a player's favorite charity or promising a particularly talented player an improved playing environment. A star pitcher, for instance, might be promised a better infield defense.

Lower ballplayer salaries would, in turn, mean lower expenses for the ballclubs. The teams could, of course, translate these lower expenses into higher club profits, but what would be the point? The team owners could never personally enjoy these higher profits. They would face the same annual maximum wage limits their ballplayers face.

So what would teamowners do? They could invest their new-found surplus in ballpark renovations. They could lower prices on tickets and hot dogs. They could donate equipment to local youth baseball leagues. They could raise the salaries of their ground crews.

Some owners—rich people who bought their clubs for tax write-offs and speculation—probably wouldn't want to play ball by the new Ten Times Rule. These profit-hungry owners might seek to unload their clubs and exit the baseball business altogther. Good riddance to them. Baseball fans can't stand quick-buck owners anyway. How many hearts, after all, did Walter O'Malley break when he pulled the Dodgers out of Brooklyn to seek more profitable pastures in Los Angeles?

In Ten Times Rule America, owners would have no incentive to break fan hearts. Moving the Dodgers made Walter O'Malley a huge new fortune. With the Ten Times Rule in place, moving franchises would no longer create huge new fortunes. Any windfall from a move—or from the sale of a franchise to a new owner in a new city—would simply be taxed away. With no incentive to move or to sell, owners would either stay put or sell out to local interests more eager to play by the Ten Times Rule.

Owners frustrated by the Ten Times Rule would be in for one last surprise if they did indeed try to unload their ballclubs and get out of the baseball business. In Ten Times Rule America, unhappy owners wouldn't find many rich people willing—or able—to pay the price they paid to get into baseball. Why? We can't answer this question without broadening our focus on Ten Times Rule America. We need to swing from baseball to bequests.

If Congress enacted the Ten Times Rule, multi-million dollar annual salaries would go the way of cheap homeruns in the Polo Grounds.

A Multi-Millionaire's Story

Let us consider the story of Walter, a typical, aging multi-millionaire in Ten Times Rule America. Walter has been grouchy ever since the Ten Times Rule was enacted. The Ten Times Rule has limited his income to $160,000 a year—in 1990 dollars—and he hasn't been happy about that. But Walter isn't totally distraught. He still has a hefty bank account, a duplex in mid-Manhattan, a mansion in Southampton, a cottage in Palm Beach, a Rolls, and a portfolio of stocks and bonds, bought for a wink and a nod and now worth a cool million or two.

Watching TV one day—the third anniversary celebration of the Ten Times Rule—Walter suffers a heart attack and passes from us. At Walter's funeral, his three grown children grieve appropriately and then make an alarming discovery. The inheritances they were so eagerly awaiting, it turns out, will do them precious little good.

Take that stock portfolio, for instance. Walter has thoughtfully left all his stocks to son Maxwell. But poor Maxwell won't be able to keep any dividends from these stocks because his income is already at the Ten Times Rule ceiling. Any dividends Maxwell receives will simply be taxed away.

And those bonds that Walter left his dear daughter Abigail? Abigail could sell those bonds and clear a huge capital gain. But she and her husband are at the Ten Times income ceiling, too. Any money they might clear from selling the stock would simply be taxed away.

But the real headaches are those fixed assets the old man so proudly cherished. Son Eliot inherits the mansion in Southampton, a truly classic abode. But Eliot already has a summer getaway of his own—and two college-age kids with Ivy League tuitions. Eliot has been working hard to maintain the style of life to which he has always been accustomed. But keeping up appearances isn't easy within the confines of the Ten Times Rule, and the last thing Eliot needs is another expense, which is just what the Southampton mansion would be. Eliot does some fast calculations: the Southampton property tax, the landscaping fees, the water bill, the air conditioning. On $160,000 a year— we're still working with those 1990 numbers—Eliot and his wife simply can't afford to maintain the Southampton place, not on top of all their other expenses. To make matters worse, the old man's Rolls is sitting in the Southampton driveway. The car insurance alone costs a fortune.[1]

Eliot, by now nearly frantic, regains his composure enough to ask his father's tax attorney for advice. Isn't there anything he can do? The lawyer shakes his head. Under the Ten Times Rule, inheritances just aren't what they used to be. Eliot could sell the house in Southampton, the lawyer notes, but any profit Eliot makes from the sale would be subject to the Ten Times Rule maximum wage. Eliot would be better off donating the house to charity. Southampton, the lawyer notes, has needed a halfway house for recovering alcoholics for some time now.

This turn of events, of course, would be unlikely to take place exactly this way—even if the Ten Times Rule were the law of the land. Aging multi-millionaires like Walter would do everything they could to keep their money out of those impersonal IRS hands, mainly by leaving their wealth to people and institutions the Ten Times Rule couldn't touch.

Instead of leaving their fortunes to already rich relations— who couldn't keep the money anyway—multi-millonaires would divvy up their treasure among those institutions and people who could keep it. Walter, being of sound mind and body, wouldn't drop his fortune in the hands of Maxwell, Abigail, and Eliot. In Ten Times Rule America, he would be much more apt to leave his millions directly to his alma mater and an assortment of his favorite charities, with maybe a couple hundred thousand or so set aside for his long-loyal chauffeur and his beloved fifth-grade teacher.

Over the span of a generation, similar scenarios would unfold every time a wealthy patriarch—or matriarch—passes on. Under

In Ten Times Rule America, inheritances wouldn't be what they used to be. Aging multi-millionaires would no longer leave their fortunes to already rich relations.

the pressures of the Ten Times Rule, billons of dollars in personal fortunes would be redistributed, some to individuals not yet at the maximum income level and others to "civil society," that network of groups and institutions so essential to the vitality of American life.

Just how much money are we talking about here? How many billions would be redistributed under the pressure of the Ten Times Rule? In 1986, according to federal estate tax statisticians, there were 80,500 Americans worth at least $5 million. Their total wealth: $990 billion.[2]

If the Ten Times Rule were law, this entire $990 billion would be rechanneled out of the hands of the super-rich and their immediate heirs. Some of this $990 billion would flow into the federal treasury, as interest and dividends from bequests swell the incomes of long-loyal chaffeurs and beloved fifth grade teachers to higher Ten Times Rule tax brackets. Other billions would fuel an enormous flowering of civic life. Foundations, schools and universities, social service agencies, and charitable institutions of every kind would all find themselves awash with contributions at levels never before imaginable. And all these contributions would be a direct byproduct of the Ten Times Rule.

Creating Wealth Under the Ten Times Rule

One generation into Ten Times Rule America, rich people—filthy rich multi-millionaires—would be an endangered species, which brings us back to baseball and those frustrated owners looking to unload their ballclubs. Who would buy these clubs once their owners put them up on the auction block?

Good question. In Ten Times Rule America, as fortunes

splinter, fewer and fewer individuals would be able to afford ballclubs. With no individual buyers to be found, new categories of owners would likely emerge. Some clubs might fall into municipal hands. Others might be sold to broad partnerships. In any case, the era of ego-tripping ownership by unaccountable rich individuals would be as dead as the dead-ball.

Skeptics on the value of the Ten Times Rule will no doubt concede this point. If the Ten Times Rule were law, they will acknowledge, there wouldn't be any multi-millionaires around to impose their petty tyrannies on the rest of us. No one, the skeptics will point out, can doubt the capacity of the Ten Times Rule to *break up* wealth. But breaking up wealth, these skeptics will argue, is not in itself a social good. What counts is the ability to *create* wealth. Any society that ceases to create wealth will eventually cannibalize itself—and leave everyone poorer. The Ten Times Rule, to be a vehicle for progress, must help create wealth.

> *Any society that ceases to create wealth will eventually leave everyone poorer. The Ten Times Rule, to be a vehicle for progress, must help create wealth.*

A point well-taken. Breaking up wealth is not enough. Indeed, breaking up wealth, if such action undermines society's capacity to create wealth, would leave us worse off than when we began.

Would the Ten Times Rule help create wealth? This is a question we simply cannot avoid.

Our answer must start with a look at the pre-eminent institution in American economic life, the corporation. What would the enactment of the Ten Times Rule mean for the American corporation?

We could, of course, give a glib answer. Given the current state of the American corporation, we could argue, how could a Ten Times Rule possibly make things any worse?

These are not salad days for American business. Library shelves are groaning under the weight of books that blast corporate America as uncompetitive, lazy, washed-up, and dumb—and some of the most biting critiques are from *inside* the corporate world. Corporations, charge insiders and outsiders alike, are overly bureaucratic institutions, trapped in hierarchical pyramids, incapable of the rapid change essential to success in modern markets. To become more productive and more competitive, the critics maintain, corporations must attack hierarchy head-on.

But American corporations, as we have seen, have failed miserably in the campaign against hierarchy. American business has proved unable to dismantle bureaucratic structures that undermine the corporate capacity to compete effectively, to be productive, to create wealth.

What makes corporate hierarchies so resilient against the forces of change? In a word: compensation. Hierarchies may no longer serve any *legitimate* business function, as business analysts so often note. But hierarchies do prop up, quite nicely, the ridiculously high compensation packages of top corporate executives. Any serious campaign against corporate hierarchy that doesn't also confront the structure of corporate compensation is simply doomed to failure.

So conclude both Peter Drucker and John Kenneth Galbraith, two of America's most widely read business commentators. Both Drucker and Galbraith argue that corporate vitality demands a maximum wage on executive compensation. A "published corporate policy that fixes the maximum compensation of all corporate executives" would be "the most radical, but also the most necessary, innovation," notes Drucker. These maximums, Drucker adds, should be set "as a multiple of the after-tax income of the lowest paid regular full-time employee."[3]

Drucker proposes a 15-to-1 ratio for small business and a 25-to-1 ratio for larger enterprises. He would make exceptions for a "star" supersalesperson or "the scientist in the lab who comes up with half a dozen highly profitable research breakthroughs" or someone "who makes a truly extraordinary contribution."[4] Galbraith simply wants firms "to specify the maximum range between average and maximum compensation."[5]

If maximums were set as Drucker and Galbraith suggest, analyst Paul Wachtel points out, corporations would reap immediate benefits. With incomes capped, Wachtel explains, corporations would no longer be able to offer astronomical salaries to attract desired individuals. Instead, corporations would have to lure talented candidates with other incentives. Corporations might actually have to demonstrate that they are structured to help candidates accomplish the tasks the corporations want to achieve. "Such a framework for attracting desired individuals would seem to be not only likely to promote a more egalitarian distribution of income but to be more efficient as well," notes Wachtel, "for it would motivate those within the organization to remove internal obstacles to the achieving of tasks."[6]

A maximum wage in corporate America would also encourage the free and candid exchange of information that hierarchies stifle, an exchange essential to competitive success in the modern market. A worker earning one-half the salary of a corporate higher-up is much more likely to have an open relationship with that higher-up than a worker earning just a small fraction of the higher-up's salary.[7] The closer the wage levels, the less likely workers would be to defer to the opinions of their "superiors." The less deference, the more dialogue—dialogue that can help solve corporate problems and identify opportunities. The end result? A

> *A maximum wage in corporate America would encourage the free and candid exchange of information that hierarchies stifle, an exchange essential to competitive success.*

better organization. A more productive company.

The maximum wage would likely have a variety of other positive effects on corporate life. With a maximum wage in effect, money previously devoted to colossal executive salary packages would suddenly become available for other purposes. Corporations could, to be sure, simply shift the dollars formerly devoted to excessive executive compensation into dividends for rich stockholders. But why bother? Higher dividends would do rich stockholders no more good than high compensation would do rich executives. In Ten Times Rule America, the income that the richest Americans receive above the maximum wage would simply be taxed away.

This Ten Times Rule reality would ease much of the pressure now on corporations to maintain high dividend levels—at the expense of other more valuable corporate expenditures. Instead of rewarding already well-rewarded rich people, corporations might actually find themselves investing more in research and development or cleaning up their environmental act or developing better training programs or improving wages, hours, and working conditions.

Old habits would, of course, die hard. CEOs and corporate boards of directors accustomed to comforting the comfortable wouldn't suddenly turn public-spirited. But what would inevitably and suddenly change under the Ten Times Rule would be the incentives that encourage, even force, executives to resist change. In contemporary America, executives earning millions in corporate compensation have a quite natural proclivity to oppose any reordering of corporate priorities that might endanger their millions. Executives whose income is capped by a maximum wage might be able to take a more sober look at the corporate agenda, particularly if pressured to do so by the unions and communities their corporation directly impacts.

What could America do, Ralph Nader once asked, "to direct corporate resources toward respecting the values and pleas that are beyond the balance sheet morality?"[8] America could enact the Ten Times Rule. No other single step would do more to make corporations more responsible organizations. Or more productive. In Ten Times Rule America, corporations would invest more in research and development, in training, in safer workplaces, in wages and working conditions, in all the prerequisites for higher and lasting productivity. The Ten Times Rule would set off a chain-reaction of side-effects that would leave corporations better able to compete and *create* wealth.

The Ten Times Rule would have an equally significant wealth-enhancing impact on the overall economy that sustains corporate America. By taxing away the excess income of rich people and lowering taxes on everyone else, the Ten Times Rule would, in effect, transfer huge amounts of wealth from the rich to the non-rich. That transfer would have an immediate stimulative impact on the economy.

Let's illustrate this impact with a picture—any picture worthy enough to hang on a museum wall. Rich people like to purchase this sort of picture. They pay millions for Rembrandts and Van Goghs. The rest of us don't buy Rembrandts. Our big-ticket items are more likely to be refrigerators. What stimulates the economy more: a rich person who spends $1 million for a Rembrandt or 1,000 non-rich people who buy frost-free refrigerators? Which expenditure creates more jobs? Which creates more wealth in society at large?

The Ten Times Rule, by transferring dollars from the rich to

> *Under the Ten Times Rule, corporations would invest more in research, in training, in safer workplaces, in wages, in all the prerequisites for higher and lasting productivity.*

the rest of us, would, as the economists like to say, enhance mass purchasing power. That would mean a greater demand for goods and services, and that would mean a healthier economy.

The Ten Times Rule would have another, more subtle wealth-enhancing impact on the economy. Under the Ten Times Rule, speculation—and the corporate havoc it wreaks—would be steadily smothered.

Let's return again to Walter, our dead-and-buried multi-millionaire. In Walter's estate is a thick portfolio of stocks and bonds. The portfolio goes to Maxwell and Abigail, who are tickled pink—until they realize that those stocks and bonds aren't going to do them very much good. Maxwell and Abigail are already at the maximum income limit. Any dividend income they receive would simply be taxed away. Maxwell and Abigail could, of course, sell their inherited stocks and bonds. But the profits would also be at-risk for the Ten Times tax. What do Walter's heirs do? They do nothing. They simply hold on to their inherited portfolios. The stocks and bonds in these portfolios become their economic security blanket for the future.

All across the United States, Maxwell and Abigail's very rich friends would face similar decisions. They would likely make the same choice. Slowly but steadily, stability would return to the stock market as the very rich lose interest in wheeling and dealing. This stability would set off another Ten Times Rule chain reaction. With the speculative temperature of the market falling, takeover artists would find fewer and fewer wealthy stockholders eager to sell and "make a big killing." The takeover frenzy of the 1980s would fade from Wall Street memories.

And that would be good news for America's economic health. The speculative 1980s left huge corporations in the hands of wild-eyed entrepreneurs who financed their takeovers by selling junk bonds. To find buyers for these unstable bonds, the entrepreneurs had to offer high interest rates. To raise the cash necessary to pay those rates, the entrepreneurs had several choices, all bad. They could close their newly acquired plants and lay off workers. They could slash research and development. They could cut corners on environmental safety. Or they could chop up their newly acquired companies, selling off divisions to raise badly needed cash, in the process often undermining marketplace competition since the buyers were often competitors. And companies that wanted to *avoid* takeover by wild-eyed entrepreneurs faced the very same choices—if they wanted to raise the cash necessary to buy up their stock and fend off takeover attacks.

In Ten Times Rule America, this cannibalistic feeding frenzy would be no more. The Ten Times Rule, by eroding incentives for speculation, would leave Wall Street considerably calmer. Stock prices, in fact, might even fall as would-be speculators lose interest and the demand for stocks drops. These lower prices, in turn, would make companies more inviting takeover targets for the one group not turned off by stock market stability: employees.

Current employee efforts to "take over" their companies usually flounder because employee groups simply can't afford the necessary financing. In Ten Times Rule America, with stock prices lower and more stable, employee takeover attempts would be far more viable.

That would be more good news for the economy. Employee takeovers are the one category of corporate takeover that makes eminent economic sense. In employee-owned companies, employees work directly for their own interests, not to feather some distant corporate nest, and this self-interest fosters higher

> *In Ten Times Rule America, lower stock prices would make companies more inviting takeover targets for the one group not turned off by stock market stability: employees.*

productivity for the individual employee-owned company. The end result for society at large? Greater wealth—thanks to the Ten Times Rule.

The Ten Times Rule and Poor People

We have talked here a great deal about the Ten Times Rule's capacity to create wealth. But what about the Ten Times Rule's ability to fight poverty? What would the Ten Times Rule offer the nation's poorest citizens?

Plenty. Money, as homespun economists like to say, is like manure. It only does any good when you spread it around. The Ten Times Rule would spread it around. The Ten Times Rule would do that spreading in many ways, most importantly by creating a constant upward pressure on the minimum wage. Under the Ten Times Rule, the minimum wage would finally do what its original supporters hoped it would do: provide, as Congressman Maury Maverick of Texas put it in 1937, "a minimum standard of decency."[9]

Today's minimum wage doesn't come close. In April 1991, the minimum wage moved to $4.25 an hour, a level that leaves the minimum wage worker of 1991 with less purchasing power than the minimum wage worker enjoyed in 1979. At $4.25 an hour, a single parent supporting two children does not earn enough to escape from poverty.

Politicians who oppose increases in the minimum wage claim their opposition reflects the best interest of poor people. Higher minimum wages, they argue, mean fewer jobs. Supporters of higher minimums, of course, vociferously disagree:

Raising the minimum wage is one of the few economic policy options that bears little cost to society as a whole but brings tremendous benefits. An increase in the minimum wage will reduce poverty, raise living standards across the board, increase the tax base, reduce welfare expenditures, boost consumer demand, and lead to more rapid economic growth.[10]

In Ten Times Rule America, even the unfeelingest opponent of the minimum wage would suddenly see the virtue in this position. Under the Ten Times Rule, the forces lobbying for a higher minimum wage, historically only a long-struggling band of labor unions and anti-poverty activists, would become a national army

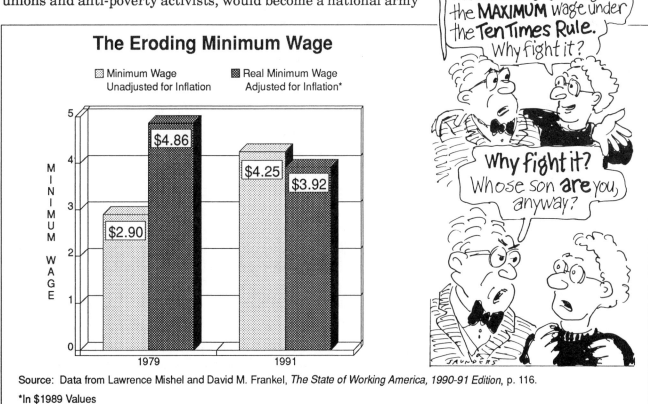

The Eroding Minimum Wage

Minimum Wage
Unadjusted for Inflation

Real Minimum Wage
Adjusted for Inflation*

1979: $2.90, $4.86

1991: $4.25, $3.92

Source: Data from Lawrence Mishel and David M. Frankel, *The State of Working America, 1990-91 Edition*, p. 116.

*In $1989 Values

Let me explain it to you Mister College Boy. The **HIGHER** the Minimum Wage, the **FEWER** lower-paying **jobs** will be available to the **poor**.

But Pop... the **HIGHER** the minimum wage, the higher the **MAXIMUM** wage under the Ten Times Rule. Why fight it?

Why fight it? Whose son **are** you, anyway?

of eager conscripts. If the Ten Times Rule were in effect, no American, not even the most comfortably self-centered yuppie, could afford to neglect the needs of the minimum wage worker.

To understand why, we need to review the Ten Times Rule arithmetic. In our earlier calculations for 1990, we assumed a $4 minimum wage. Based on that minimum, the maximum annual income for a single taxpayer would be $80,000, ten times the annual wage of a minimum wage worker.

But what if the minimum wage were $5? The annual minimum wage would then be $200 a week, $10,000 for a 50-week working year. The maximum annual income for a single taxpayer would suddenly jump to $100,000, a 25 percent boost in allowable income for those at the top of the income scale.

But it's not just the wealthy—or the poor—who would benefit immediately from a higher minimum wage under the Ten Times Rule. All taxpayers would benefit. Under the Ten Times Rule, for instance, a single taxpayer earning $48,000 would pay 6 percent of that income in federal taxes if the minimum wage were $4 an hour—because $48,000 would be six times $8,000, the annual minimum wage when the minimum hourly rate is $4.

But if the minimum wage were $5 an hour, then the minimum annual wage would be $10,000, and income of $48,000 would be less than five times the minimum annual income. Any single taxpayer earning $48,000 would, in this situation, pay taxes at only a 4 percent rate.

Under the Ten Times Rule, in other words, every advance for the have-nots would become, automatically, an advance for the haves. Such a dynamic could profoundly transform national politics. The greedy would become the champions of the needy.

All this upward pressure on the minimum wage would be one

way the Ten Times Rule would spread the wealth. There would be others.

Under the Ten Times Rule, as we have seen, whatever income rich people earn above the maximum wage simply disappears into the federal treasury. But rich people aren't going to simply dump their excess good fortune into the federal coffers. Sooner or later, they'll start realizing that if they're going to be parted from their money anyway, they might as well get some credit for the parting. The Ten Times Rule would, as a result, spark a surge of charitable contributions.

But don't the rich already give fortunes to charities, without the pressure of the Ten Times Rule? In fact, they do not. The richer a person is, the lower the percentage of income that person is likely to donate to charity. In 1990, economist Robert Reich points out, American households with incomes less than $10,000 contributed 5.5 percent of their earnings to charities or religious organizations. Households earning more than $100,000 a year gave away only 2.9 percent. Between 1980 and 1988, glory days for rich people, "taxpayers earning $500,000 or more slashed their average donations to $16,062 in 1988 from $47,432 in 1980."[11]

"Anybody who spends any appreciable length of time in the company of the rich becomes accustomed to their peculiar coldness," writes Lewis Lapham. "Once money comes to be understood as the staff of life, obviously nobody has enough of it to squander on anybody other than oneself."[12]

The Ten Times Rule would help melt that coldness. And if the Ten Times Rule didn't make rich people more charitably inclined, that wouldn't matter, for the Ten Times Rule, by lowering taxes on everybody but the rich, would leave more and more money in the hands of non-rich people, who are much warmer—and more

If the Ten Times Rule were in effect, no American, not even the most comfortably self-centered yuppie, could afford to neglect the needs of the minimum wage worker.

willing to donate to good causes—than the rich.

Giving Rich People an Out

Are all these societal benefits from the Ten Times Rule too good to be true? Surely there must be a loophole to all this. After all, in years past, every effort ever made to tax the rich has floundered on loopholes. Surely loopholes would emerge in Ten Times Rule America, clever outs that rich people would be able to use to keep income above the Ten Times limit.

Yes, loopholes would undoubtedly emerge in Ten Times Rule America. But if we were smart, we wouldn't wait for loopholes to emerge. We would actually build a loophole into the Ten Times law right from the start. Our loophole of choice would be state and local government bonds.

Under current federal income tax law, any income earned from state and local bonds is tax-free. You can "clip coupons" to your heart's delight and not pay a cent of income tax on the bond income you receive.

In Ten Times Rule America, income from state and local bonds would continue to be tax-exempt—and that would make state and local bonds the only investment "loophole" to the Ten Times Rule. Rich people, of course, would rush to shove their fortunes through this loophole. The demand for state and local bonds would soar.

This rising demand would place state and local governments squarely in the driver's seat. In a sellers' market, state and local governments wouldn't have to offer 7 or 8 percent interest to attract potential bondholders. Instead, states and localities would be able to offer much lower returns, maybe only 2 or 3 percent, and still find a steady supply of eager buyers. With these lower interest obligations, borrowing would become a much less expensive proposition for state and local governments. States and localities would suddenly find themselves able to afford badly needed projects that, in the past, would have been far too expensive to consider. In short order, the tax-exempt bond "loophole" to the Ten Times Rule would spark a wide range of state and local government projects to rebuild America's decaying infrastructure: new schools, new water purification plants, new bridges, new transit lines. These new projects would mean new jobs, more income for working people, a healthier economy, more tax revenues for state and local governments, better government services. Once again, a Ten Times Rule chain reaction.

> *By pushing bond interest rates down, the Ten Times Rule would spark a wide range of state and local projects to rebuild America's decaying infrastructure.*

And what about our rich people? Would their tax-exempt income from state and local bonds undermine the concept of a maximum wage? Not much. At a 2 percent rate of return, a wealthy individual would have to buy a million dollars worth of bonds to earn $20,000 worth of tax-free income. Fine. This $20,000 would be a small price for the rest of us to pay for access to that $1 million.

The state and local bond "loophole" would benefit the non-rich majority in other ways as well. If rich people knock themselves out to buy state and local bonds—and generate a demand that drives interest rates on these bonds ever lower—then all interest rates would sink. In Ten Times Rule America, lower interest rates would come quickly to the banking industry. With bonds paying only 2 or 3 percent, banks would be able to attract savers with 3 or 4 percent rates, which means that banks could then offer mortgages at 4 or 5 percent—and make housing more affordable. More chain reaction.

Let's linger a moment on housing in Ten Times Rule America.

Today, only 9 percent of Americans who currently rent can afford to buy homes of their own. Homeownership, the Census Bureau has concluded, is "not within the reach of the vast majority of people who did not buy prior to the price run-ups of the 1970s and 1980s."[13] If mortgage costs don't shut a family out of the housing market, sales prices will. The Ten Times Rule would totally change all that.

Remember Eliot, Walter's son who inherited that mansion in Southampton. Eliot, to his chagrin, found that he couldn't afford to maintain the mansion. He already had a big house of his own and a variety of other demands on his maximum wage family income.

In Ten Times Rule America, there would be many Eliots, rich people who inherit property that they can't possibly afford to maintain. What would these Eliots do? Some would dump their luxury property on the housing market, but, with the Ten Times Rule in effect, these Eliots wouldn't find many buyers, at least not at the high prices the properties were once worth. More chain reaction. Prices would fall on luxury properties. If luxury properties are selling for less, then property owners trying to sell real estate just below luxury status would have to lower their prices, too. They would have no choice. Buyers wouldn't purchase a near-luxury home if they could get a luxury home at the same price. The Ten Times Rule, in short, would rapidly bring housing prices back to affordability.

Our Character and the Ten Times Rule

Housing. Education. The environment. In every social sphere we examine, the Ten Times Rule would exert a clear and strong positive impact on American society. But what about the Ten Times Rule impact on individuals? Would the Ten Times Rule help us become "better people"? Or would the Ten Times Rule, by limiting the amount of money people can earn, undermine the work ethic and leave America directionless and lazy?

Critics of the Ten Times Rule would, of course, make the latter claim again and again if a campaign for a Ten Times Rule ever became a serious threat to the well-being of the wealthy. Would they be right? Would the Ten Times Rule undermine the work ethic? It's difficult to see how. The vast majority of Americans—99 percent—would be untouched by the Ten Times Rule income cap. For the average American family, the chances of earning $160,000 a year—the Ten Times cap were the minimum wage $4 an hour—are about as likely as winning the lottery. You can't crush incentive in America by capping income at a level most Americans can't even dream of reaching.

And those few Americans who would have their incomes capped by the Ten Times Rule, what about them? Some would sulk. But others might wise up and see the Ten Times cap not as a limit, but as a liberation.

In Ten Times Rule America, wealthy workaholics—"people whose high income is earned by extraordinary effort"—would have no reason to continue their anti-social approach to life. With no rational excuse left for whiling away every waking hour at work, these poor souls might re-examine the mindless money-chasing patterns of their lives.[14]

These maximum-waged people might discover that money isn't the only incentive, that there is joy in working with others for the common good, be that work counseling in a rape crisis center or calculating church finances. Millions of their non-rich

> *The Ten Times Rule might prompt some wealthy workaholics to re-examine the mindless money-chasing patterns of their lives.*

neighbors have already made this discovery.

"Not only do Americans do more work without pay than they do with pay," notes Philip Slater, "but what they do is probably, on balance, better done, more useful, and less destructive than what they get paid to do."[15]

The Ten Times Rule might also liberate rich people—all people, in fact—to look very differently at their career choices. How many corporate wheeler-dealers are frustrated painters or cabinet makers? In contemporary America, a culture where winning is defined by the amount of money accumulated, our society's most competitive—and sometimes most talented—people cannot afford to let their hearts direct how they choose their livelihoods. But in Ten Times Rule America "winning" would take on new meaning. A successful individual in one field of endeavor would make a salary comparable to a successful individual's salary in any other field. In Ten Times Rule America, for instance, top corporate executives would make salaries comparable to a school district superintendent, not 30 times as much as they currently do.

Sound far-fetched? It shouldn't. In Japan, the chairman of a prefectural school board, the equivalent of a superintendent in a large American county school district, only makes two or three times less than the typical executive in a large Japanese corporation. Education, not so coincidentally, occupies an honored place in Japanese life, not the second class status accorded education in the United States.[16] Why can't we learn from that? Why must our society's reward structure steer people away from noble occupations so essential to our culture and our future? Why can't we do better than that?

We can do better, if we relegate the pursuit of the all-mighty dollar to a less exalted plane. As economist John Maynard Keynes noted over a half-century ago, "when the accumulation of wealth is no longer of high social importance," we "shall be able to rid ourselves of many of the pseudo-moral principles which have hagridden us for two hundred years, by which we have exalted some of the most distasteful of human qualities into the position of the highest values."[17]

An Alternate Scenario

We have assumed, in all our discussion to this point, that the Ten Times Rule would work as intended. In Ten Times Rule America, we have assumed, rich people would either hand the IRS all their incomes above the maximum wage or channel some of that excess income into charitable contributions and tax-free government bonds. Both these options would be socially acceptable in Ten Times Rule America.

But what if rich people didn't follow the Ten Times Rule script? What if they engaged in socially unacceptable—and even downright illegal—behaviors? What if they cheated on their taxes? What if they tried to spite the IRS by giving away all their income to charity? What if they just picked up and left the country, taking their ample incomes with them?

What then? If rich people didn't pay their Ten Times Rule taxes, wouldn't that leave the U.S. Treasury empty and force tax hikes on average Americans? And wouldn't those tax hikes on average Americans erode their purchasing power and drive the economy into recession or worse? Wouldn't those hard times spell the end of Ten Times Rule America?

Ten Times Rule America would, without a doubt, have no choice but to assume and expect the *worst* from rich people. The

Maximum-waged people might discover that money isn't the only incentive, that there is joy in working with others for the common good.

well-endowed would have little reason to cooperate with Ten Times Rule America and every reason to spite it. But how much damage could rich people really do in Ten Times Rule America, even if they put their minds to it?

Could cheating by rich people, for instance, deny the IRS significant amounts of Ten Times Rule tax dollars? Not likely.

In Ten Times Rule America, the vast majority of Americans would have little incentive to cheat on their taxes—because their taxes would be so much lower than they are now. The IRS, as a result, would be able to concentrate its enforcement resources on the less than 1 percent of the population that *would* have an incentive to cheat: the very rich.

In these enforcement efforts, the IRS could count on considerable public support. In Ten Times Rule America, the public would have little tolerance or sympathy for people who cheat on their taxes. Tax cheaters in Ten Times Rule America wouldn't be hard-working people desperately trying to make ends meet, or average citizens justifiably angry about an unfair tax burden. Ten Times Rule tax cheaters would be filthy rich taxpayers out to sabotage a new economic order that benefits everyone who isn't filthy rich.

In Ten Times Rule America, in short, cheating on taxes would be a high-risk behavior for any rich people so bold and foolish to try.

What about charitable contributions? Couldn't rich people spite the IRS by giving away huge portions of their incomes to charity and deducting those contributions from taxes due? After all, if the government would be getting any income over the maximum wage anyway, why wouldn't rich people choose to give their money to a recipient of their choice, instead of the hated IRS?

In Ten Times Rule America, rich people could indeed give away all the income they wanted. But their charitable contributions wouldn't eliminate their tax obligations. The federal tax code currently limits the amount of charitable deductions a taxpayer can claim in any one year. Ten Times Rule America might choose to simply continue current limits or set new ones.

What might that mean for a wealthy taxpayer who gives away $1 million in income to spite the IRS? If the charitable deduction limit were 50 percent, our wealthy taxpayer would still owe the IRS $500,000. To meet this tax obligation, the taxpayer would have to liquidate personal wealth—by dumping stocks, selling a house, or cashing out a life insurance policy or two.

Charitable giving, it seems clear, would pose little threat to the fiscal stability of Ten Times Rule America. If charitable contributions from the wealthy did significantly dent tax revenues, Ten Times Rule America could simply limit the size of charitable deductions.

Too scared to cheat, unable to spite the IRS by giving income away, why wouldn't rich people in Ten Times Rule America simply leave the country—and take their money with them?

Some rich people would undoubtedly take the money and run. Ten Times Rule America could, of course, limit capital flight, by making it illegal for rich people to exit the United States with any assets above a certain amount. Other nations have at times imposed capital flight limits, with varying degrees of success. In the modern electronic international economy, such limits aren't easy to enforce.

In truth, if rich people wanted to leave, there would be little a democratic Ten Times Rule America could do to stop them. But rich people would pay a price for leaving, even if there were no

In Ten Times Rule America, cheating on taxes would be a high-risk behavior for any rich person so bold and foolish to try.

capital flight limits.

If, for instance, rich people attempted from abroad to hang on to their wealth-producing assets in the United States—their stock portfolios, their properties, their businesses—any dividends, rents, and capital gains due them would be subject to the same Ten Times tax rates they sought to escape. If they sat back in their foreign tax haven and refused to pay the Ten Times taxes due, the IRS would seize the assets.

If our wealthy refugees decided instead to sell their assets in the United States, they would still be liable for taxes on any profits from the sale. Couldn't wealthy refugees, safe in their Swiss bunkers, just stiff the IRS on any taxes due? Not if the IRS required stockbrokers and real estate agents to withhold tax dollars from sales proceeds, in much the same way the IRS already requires racetracks to withhold tax dollars from any huge windfalls won by lucky bettors.

For rich people, all these factors add up to some significant economic disincentives to leaving. Rich people who left would still have to pay Ten Times Rule taxes on their income-producing assets in the United States. If they sold those assets, they would have to pay Ten Times Rule taxes on the sale profits. And if they tried to sell out and flee the United States in that brief window of opportunity after the Ten Times Rule was enacted but before it went into effect, they would probably find themselves selling at fire sale rates, as their fellow rich Americans the nation over panicked and also rushed to sell.

But the real disincentive for would-be wealthy refugees would be cultural, not economic. Some rich people might be able to find eternal happiness on the Riviera or a ranch in Costa Rica. Many more probably would not. European television does run clips from

NFL football games, but how many Texas oilmen could be happy knowing someone else was sitting in their Dallas Cowboys skybox? Rich people wouldn't leave Ten Times Rule en masse. They just couldn't. In Ten Times Rule America, rich people would see their take-home incomes shrivel to a fraction of their former size. But rich people would eventually learn to live with that shriveled income. After all, even shriveled, they would still be the richest people in America.

Back to our original question: Could rich people sabotage Ten Times Rule America? They could try. They would try. But they wouldn't get far.

Almost Heaven?

Let's not get totally carried away here. The Ten Times Rule would make an enormous positive contribution to the well-being of the American people. But the Ten Times Rule would not cure all the problems that plague us. The enactment of the Ten Times Rule wouldn't automatically erase discrimination or stop attacks against the environment or insure quality education or even guarantee homes for the homeless.

But a campaign for a Ten Times Rule could make Americans sit up and pay attention to politics and public policy again—and that would be no small feat in an era when over half the nation's adults routinely find no reason to vote. A campaign for a Ten Times Rule could be the spark that stirs America's couch-potato soul. And if the Ten Times Rule were, through some unimaginable miracle, enacted, then real democratic politics could begin, a politics undistorted by the great power of wealth, a politics that tries to come to grips with issues that really count.

A campaign for the Ten Times Rule could make Americans sit up and pay attention to politics again—no small feat in an era when half of America sees no reason to vote.

Is a miracle indeed what we're talking about here? Is a political miracle the only conceivable way the Ten Times Rule could become the law of the land? Or is the enactment of a Ten Times Rule within the ballpark of our political imagination? Can we imagine a scenario, a turn of events, that might actually make the Ten Times Rule the law of the land?

Let's try.

Notes

1. How much does maintaining a rich and famous lifestyle actually cost? In 1991, New York real estate developer Peter Kalikow filed bankruptcy court papers that offer a fascinating glimpse at what the wealthy consider "operating expenses." From the properties he had placed into bankruptcy, Kalikow asked the court to allow him: $65,142 to staff his $6 million house in Montauk, $74,034 for the crew of his $8.5 million yacht, $71,400 in maintenance fees for his $3.8 million Manhattan triplex, $30,348 for upkeep on his boat, $26,370 for car insurance, and assorted other expenses that added up to $435,084—just enough for six months of life in the fast lane.

   Richard D. Hylton, "Sometimes Those Bare Necessities Include Yacht Docking," *New York Times*, August 25, 1991, p. E5.

2. Marvin Schwartz and Barry Johnson "Estimates of Personal Wealth 1986," *Statistics of Income Bulletin*, Spring, 1990, p. 71.

3. Peter F. Drucker *The Changing World of the Executive* (New York: Times Books, 1982), p. 23-24.

4. Ibid., p 24.

5. John Kenneth Galbraith *Economics and the Public Purpose* (Boston: Houghton Mifflin Company, 1973), p. 294.

6. Paul L. Wachtel *The Poverty of Affluence* (Philadelphia: New Society Publishers, 1989), p. 282.

7. See the discussion in Martin Carnoy and Derek Shearer *Economic Democracy* (Armonk, N.Y.: M. E. Sharpe Inc., 1980), p. 316.

8. From Introduction, Morton Mintz and Jerry S. Cohen *America, Inc.: Who Owns and Operates the United States* (New York: Dell, 1971), p. 16.

9. Richard B. Henderson *Maury Maverick: A Political Biography* (Austin: University of Texas Press, 1970), p. 145.

10. *Economic Notes*, March-April 1988, pp. 12-13.

11. Robert Reich "Secession of the Successful," *New York Times Magazine*, January 20, 1991.

12. Lewis H. Lapham *Money and Class in America* (New York: Weidenfeld & Nicolson), p. 101.

13. Kirstin Downey "Fewer Renters Can Afford To Buy Home," *Washington Post*, June 14, 1991, pp. A1, A18.

14. Herbert Gans "More Equality: Income and Taxes" in Helen I. Safa and Gloria Levitas, eds., *Social Problems in Corporate America* (New York: Harper & Row, 1975), p. 337.

15. Philip Slater *Wealth Addiction* (New York: E.P. Dutton, 1980), p. 124.

16. "Executive Pay Poisons Education," *Industry Week*, July 16, 1990.

17. Robert Theobold, editor *The Guaranteed Income: Next Step in Economic Evolution?* (Garden City: Doubleday & Company, Inc., 1966), p. 86.

5. Toward a TenTimesRule

"A century ago, America in the robber-baron age was far more unequal than it is today," economist Robert Kuttner noted the day before Election Day, 1990. "But things changed—and they can change again. All it takes is political imagination."[1]

Envisioning a Ten Times Rule America takes, to say the least, political imagination. The idea that American politics, as now constituted, could ever produce a maximum wage of any sort seems incredibly far-fetched. American politics seems incapable of even inconveniencing rich people, let alone eliminating them.

A case in point: the fall 1990 tax-the-rich debate on Capitol Hill. For a month before the 1990 elections, the halls of Congress echoed with unusually sharp tax-the-rich rhetoric. Members of Congress decried the shrinking tax burden on wealthy people and loudly demanded tax justice.

In the end, after all the huffing and puffing subsided, Congress did enact legislation that raised the share of the nation's tax burden paid by those with incomes over $200,000. How much did Congress raise the tax burden share that rich people bear? Congress upped this burden *less than 1 percent.*[2] American lawmakers, it appears, are not ready to do anything more about taxing the rich than talk about it.

What about the American people? Are Americans ready for a serious campaign to redistribute income? Ready to consider limits on the income rich people receive?

These questions are not regularly posed by pollsters, but we do have some data. Back in 1976, for instance, one poll asked a national sample of Americans whether they agreed or disagreed with the following proposition: "The government should limit the amount any individual is allowed to earn in a year." The number of Americans who agreed with that statement was something less than overwhelming. Just 6 percent of blue-collar workers agreed with the proposition, a figure even lower than the 7 percent of "upper" class respondents who supported a cap on incomes.[3]

About the same time as this poll was taken, researcher Jennifer Hochschild was conducting in-depth interviews on low-, middle-, and high-income taxpayers in New Haven, Connecticut. Hochschild found public attitudes toward wealth much more complicated than poll numbers would indicate. Hochschild asked an assortment of New Haven adults to describe their vision of utopia. Most told her that utopia would be "good health, travel, a loving family, no crime." But most of Hochschild's subjects also began their utopian visions by assuming "universal material well-being and absence of divisive, corrosive differences in wealth."[4]

Do Americans want to redistribute wealth or not? Concluded Hochschild in the 1970s: "We are left with an unstable balance between support for and rejection of the status quo."[5]

That balance may have tipped somewhat in the 1980s. As the decade moved on, and the income of rich people moved up, public unease and anger about disparities in wealth slowly began to rise.

One 1989 survey, released by a North Carolina company, "found a 53 percent local majority favoring a cap on the incomes of professional athletes, corporate executives, movie stars, stock-brokers, and the like."[6] In 1990, a *Fortune* magazine poll uncovered similar attitudes. Over half the American people, *Fortune* reported, believe that "millionaires have gotten where they are by exploiting others." The number of Americans "who think society would be better off without millionaires at all," *Fortune* added, has increased since 1979 "by 11 percentage points, from one in four Americans to one in three."[7]

Some political analysts believe the United States stands on the threshold of a new epoch of "cyclical populism." American history demonstrates, says Kevin Phillips, that "excessive stratification—unprecedented concentrations of wealth on one side and diminishing prospects for another 30- to 40 percent of the population—has eventually incited political upheaval."[8]

Every previous American political upheaval against wealth, as we have noted, has fallen short. For well over a century, all attempts to limit the income and wealth of rich people have sooner or later ended in a clear reaffirmation of an inequitable status quo. Could a campaign for a Ten Times Rule ever hope to break this cycle of futility?

Perhaps. The Ten Times Rule, by explicitly linking caps on the income of the wealthy to lower taxes and a higher quality of life for everyone else, might be able to capture America's imagination far more significantly than any tax-the-rich initiatives of the past. The Ten Times Rule might be the strategic vehicle that could finally help Americans "realize that they can best achieve their own expectations if income and wealth were shared more equally."[9]

But none of this will happen, no imaginations will be captured, unless some significant social force in American life steps forward

> The Ten Times Rule, by linking caps on the incomes of the wealthy to a higher quality of life for everyone else, might be able to capture America's political imagination.

to build a foundation for a Ten Times Rule campaign. What social force could that be? The prospect list isn't very long.

The labor movement, at first glance, would seem to be the institution most likely to lay the groundwork for a Ten Times Rule campaign. Labor is, after all, the most politically potent institution in America dedicated to the struggle for economic justice. But the likelihood for labor action would not appear to be particularly high. Down through the years, the labor movement has seldom targeted the vast gaps in income that separate the rich from everyone else.

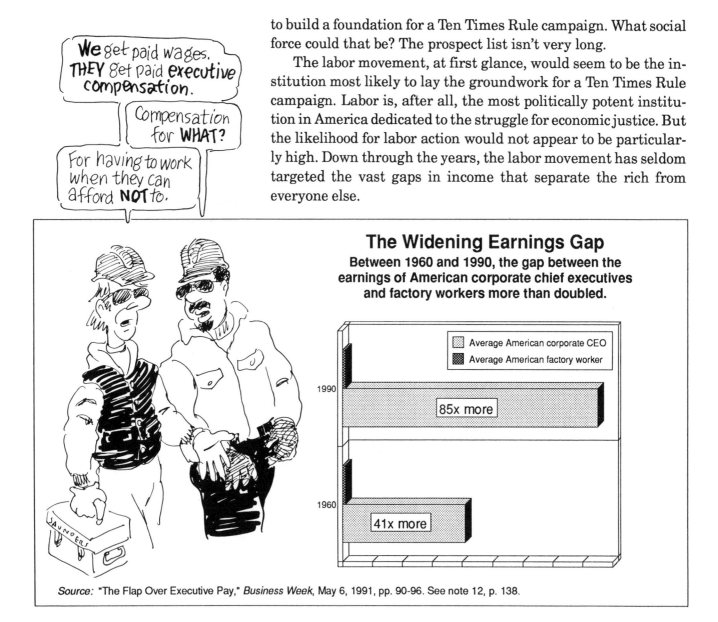

We get paid wages. **THEY** get paid **executive** compensation.

Compensation for **WHAT**?

For having to work when they can afford **NOT** to.

The Widening Earnings Gap

Between 1960 and 1990, the gap between the earnings of American corporate chief executives and factory workers more than doubled.

- Average American corporate CEO
- Average American factory worker

1990 85x more

1960 41x more

Source: "The Flap Over Executive Pay," *Business Week*, May 6, 1991, pp. 90-96. See note 12, p. 138.

"Trade unions have sought better wages, working conditions, and benefits," notes Jennifer Hochschild, "but seldom reductions in wage differentials or ties between corporate profits and wages."[10]

Instead of trying to limit the *highest* incomes, trade unions in the United States—and other nations as well—have worked diligently to raise the *lowest* incomes, by establishing effective minimum wage floors. But raising minimum incomes, while ignoring incomes at the top of the economic scale, may be a prescription for an inflation that saps working people's purchasing power, as trade union-backed governments in Portugal in the mid-1970s and Chile in the early 1980s quickly discovered. "To achieve an income redistribution without generating inflationary consequences, an intrasalary adjustment is required," note economists Martin Carnoy and Derek Shearer. *"If low wages are to be increased, they must be raised at the expense of high wages."* The American labor movement's historic position "favoring a higher minimum wage, while sidestepping or ignoring the issue of a maximum wage," Carnoy and Shearer conclude, "is self-defeating and economically wrong."[11]

Might American labor drop this historic reluctance to confront directly the income of the wealthy? The time may now be ripe for just such a confrontation, for several reasons. For starters, millions of Americans, both those who belong to unions and those who don't, have come to believe that corporate executives are paid far too much. The excesses of corporate compensation are too visible to either ignore or forget. In 1990, LIN Broadcasting's chief executive, Donald A. Pels, cleared a cool $186.2 million after his company merged with another. Time Warner's Steven J. Ross "earned" a mere $78.1 million in 1990. In 1960, the average chief executive made 41 times the income of the average factory worker. In 1990, CEOs outclipped workers by an 85-to-1 margin.[12]

But the huge inequities in corporate salary structures aren't just unfair. They make no economic sense. Trade unionists can now argue, with considerable academic support, that lower executive compensation is a prerequisite for improving the competitive posture of American corporations. Japan and Germany, as we have seen, tolerate far narrower disparities within the corporate pay structure. Those narrower pay disparities translate into leaner, more efficient corporate organizations.

American trade unions could undoubtedly count on widespread public sympathy if they made limits on executive compensation a key demand at the bargaining table. Collective bargaining, in fact, could very easily become the vehicle for introducing the Ten Times Rule into American life. No corporate executive, unions could argue, should be paid more than ten times the wage of the lowest-paid employee in the company.[13]

Unions could go on to demand that the money saved by cutting excess corporate compensation ought to be productively reinvested: in endeavors that might lead to better products or new jobs or safer, environmentally cleaner workplaces. Management, to maintain executive compensation at excessively high levels, would have to argue the indefensible: that outlandishly high corporate salaries are somehow economically "necessary"—an argument to which trade unionists could simply retort, "Not in Japan!"

Ten Times Rule debates at the bargaining table would, of course, inevitably raise the profile of the Ten Times Rule in society at large. If a Ten Times Rule makes sense for an individual corporation, more and more Americans would begin to ask, why not consider a Ten Times Rule for the nation as a whole?

But making the transition from bargaining table to broader society would be a most difficult maneuver. The bargaining table offers working people a chance to directly confront the rich people whose incomes they seek to limit. Society at large offers no comparable opportunity. At the bargaining table, working people sit as equals. In national politics, ordinary, non-rich people don't even have a seat.

The United States Senate, commentators now note with increasing frequency, has become a millionaires' club. The House of Representatives overflows with members directly dependent on rich people's campaign contributions.

"Washington is so accustomed to wealth in its midst," notes journalist Richard Harwood, "that the election of a house painter to Congress a few years back was a source of amusement."[14]

It's difficult to imagine either the House or the Senate ever enacting a Ten Times Rule. And even if a Ten Times law somehow did make its way through Congress, it's difficult to imagine the courts not undoing whatever Congress enacts. In 1894, after Congress enacted the first post-Civil War era income tax, rich people took their case to the courts. In 1895, the Supreme Court struck down the income tax as unconstitutional. With the nation's high courts now dominated by Reagan-Bush appointees, history would be eminently repeatable if a Ten Times Rule ever passed Congress.

What about the state level? Couldn't Ten Times Rule forces simply bypass the national level and work to enact Ten Times Rule legislation in individual states?

Politically, this state approach does make ample sense, mainly because the wealthy aren't evenly distributed in every state. Rich people in the United States today essentially cluster on the

> *American trade unions could undoubtedly count on widespread public sympathy if they made limits on executive compensation a key demand at the bargaining table.*

coasts and in a few oases of wealth in between. Any moves to take the wealthy on directly in these strongholds aren't likely to go very far. A Ten Times Rule would be far more likely to take root and grow in states and sections of the country where rich people *don't* congregate. The turn-of-the-century drive for a federal income tax, we need to remember, drew its initial strength from the hinterlands of the South and West, not from the millionaire-dominated East. A Ten Times Rule campaign, to be successful, would have to take a similar geographic approach. The campaign would have to begin in places where advocates for a maximum wage would face the least opposition from rich people.

But even in states where wealth is weakest, rich people hold the ultimate trump card: the threat to move. Iowa rich people faced by the prospect of a state maximum wage would simply announce their intention to move across the river into Illinois—and take their tax dollars with them. In the face of this economic blackmail, Iowa maximum wage advocates would have no choice but to relent. No single state could ever hope to make a maximum wage stick.

The strategic conclusion? A Ten Times Rule campaign must be state-based, because rich people are more politically vulnerable in some states than they are at the national level. But a Ten Times Rule campaign must also seek to enact a national maximum wage, because no single state could survive the economic blackmail rich people would immediately wage against it.

Could a Ten Times Rule campaign that focuses on action at the state level ever hope to enact a *national* maximum wage? Yes, *if* the campaign were organized as a drive to amend the U.S. Constitution.

Let's review the constitutional bidding. An amendment can

become part of the United States Constitution in one of two ways. Either Congress can, by a two-thirds majority, propose an amendment, which must then be ratified by three-quarters of the states, or two-thirds of the states must individually call for a constitutional convention. This convention could then propose the sought-after amendment, which would then have to be ratified by three-quarters of the states.

In modern times, various political causes have seen the second approach as a viable option for generating public support. Advocates of a "balance the budget" amendment, for instance, have based their entire campaign on a state-by-state constitutional amendment strategy. So far, over 30 states have endorsed the call for a balance-the-budget constitutional convention.

Ten Times Rule advocates could take the same approach and seek, one state at a time, to win legislative approval for a constitutional convention on the Ten Times Rule. The Ten Times Rule campaign emphasis would be on endorsing and electing state legislative candidates who would support a Ten Times Rule amendment to the United States Constitution.

The first states targeted for such an effort, of course, would be states where the campaign would have the greatest chance of success—not New York, not California, not Florida, not any state that rich people like to call home, but a state more like an Iowa, a Vermont, or a North Dakota. Victories, or even heated debates, in any of these states would begin to spread the Ten Times Rule message across the nation. Tactical organizing lessons learned in small state battles could then be applied to larger states. With growing savvy and numbers, Ten Times Rule advocates could begin to prevail state by state. Ten Times Rule momentum at the state level would, in turn, open new political options at the na-

> *Rich people today cluster on America's coasts and in a few oases of wealth in between. Any moves to take the wealthy on directly in these strongholds aren't likely to go far.*

tional level. Ten Times Rule successes in the states would spark Ten Times Rule congressional candidacies. The unthinkable—congressional passage of a Ten Times Rule constitutional amendment, a step that would make a constitutional convention unnecessary—might become thinkable.

The modern federal income tax, as we've noted earlier, came into effect through exactly this route. Congress adopted an income tax amendment in 1909, and that amendment then won the necessary approvals from three-quarters of the states. Once ratified, the income tax amendment became the constitutional law of the land, and a hostile Supreme Court was powerless to strike it down. Once ratified, a Ten Times Rule amendment would also be immune to court attack.

This isn't the place to fantasize the ins and outs of a campaign that could place the Ten Times Rule on the American political map. Here we need only make one point: an effective Ten Times Rule campaign isn't totally outside the realm of political possibility. In American tax history, after all, stranger things have happened. Back in 1895, for instance, after the Supreme Court struck down the 2 percent income tax enacted in 1894, "only a mad man would have dared a prophesy that within the period of the next thirty years a Federal revenue act would bring rates of 19 to 88 percent."[15] Yet that's exactly what happened, notes historian Randolph Paul. Between 1894 and World War I, the top income tax rate on the wealthy went from 2 to 88 percent.

With the Ten Times Rule in effect, the top rate on the incomes of the rich would go even higher, to 100 percent. Impossible? Why? If we as a nation once made the jump from 2 to 88 percent, why can't we now make the jump from 31 percent—the current top rate on wealthy people—to 100?

We can make this jump. A Ten Times Rule could be won. We, the vast non-rich majority, could win it.

And if we did win, America's tiny rich minority would one day thank us for the effort, for the Ten Times Rule wouldn't be about punishing any one group. The Ten Times rule would be about creating an America that works for everyone, an America where Americans "are independent but cooperative, solicitous of the needy but respectful of others' autonomy, productive but noncompetitive, equal but not identical."[16]

Utopia? No. But close enough.

Notes

1. Robert Kuttner
   "A Still-declining Middle," *Boston Globe,*
   November 5, 1990.

2. *New York Times,* October 29, 1990.

3. Kay Lehman Schlozman and Sidney
   Verba
   As quoted in Jennifer L. Hochschild,
   What's Fair?: American Beliefs about
   Distributive Justice (Cambridge: Harvard
   University Press, 1981), pp. 18-19.

4. Ibid., p. 187.

5. Ibid., p. 281.

6. Kevin Phillips
   *The Politics of Rich and Poor: Wealth and
   the American Electorate in the Reagan
   Aftermath* (New York: Random House,
   1990), p. 185.

7. Anne B. Fisher

8. "A Brewing Revolt Against the Rich,"
   Fortune, December 17, 1990, p. 90.

8. Phillips, op.cit., p. 208.

9. Safa and Levitas, op.cit., p. 334.

10. Hochschild, op.cit., p. 15.

11. Martin Carnoy and Derek Shearer
    Economic Democracy (Armonk, N.Y.: M.
    E. Sharpe Inc., 1980), p. 320-21.

12. "The Flap Over Executive Pay," *Business
    Week,* May 6, 1991, pp. 90-96. These
    ratios show a greater CEO-worker gap
    than figures on pp. 24-25. Ratio estimates
    do vary, for various statistical reasons.
    Analyst Graef Crystal argues that major
    U.S. CEOs now make 160 times the
    average worker pay. See his *In Search of
    Excess: The Overcompensation of
    American Executives* (New York: W.W.
    Norton, 1991), p. 205.

13. A recommendation noted in passing by
    Ravi Batra in his book, *The Great
    Depression of 1990* (New York: Simon &
    Schuster, 1987), p. 183. Batra makes a
    much more detailed case for the
    maximum wage concept in an earlier
    book, *PROUT: The Alternative to
    Capitalism and Marxism* (Lanham,
    Maryland: University Press of America,
    1980). See pp. 27-44.

14. Richard Harwood
    "Why We Won't Soak the Rich,"
    Washington Post, October 17, 1982.

15. Randolph E. Paul
    Taxation in the United States (Boston:
    Little, Brown and Company, 1954), p.
    701.

16. Hochschild, op.cit., p. 160.